The Struggle for the People

OVE KORSGAARD

THE
Struggle
FOR THE
People

*Five Hundred Years
of Danish History in Short*

DANISH SCHOOL OF EDUCATION PRESS

The Struggle for the People
Author: Ove Korsgaard
Copyright © Danmarks Pædagogiske Universitetsforlag and author
Typeset: BookPartnerMedia
Cover: Designkolonien, Louise Glargaard
Print: Jønsson Grafisk
Printed in Denmark 2008
1. Edition, 1. Impression
ISBN: 978-87-7684-253-6

Some of the illustrations in this book are reproduced without
permission by the copyright holder. Danish School of Education
Press has not been able to collect any information about
contacts. Please address any information to the Danish School of
Education Press.

This publication is supported by Danish-AWE.

Danish School of Education Press
Tuborgvej 164
2400 København NV
Denmark
www.forlag.dpu.dk

How to buy:
National Library of Education
P.O.Box 840, DK – 2400 Copenhagen NV
www.dpu.dk/bogsalg
bogsalg@dpu.dk
Tlf.: +45 8888 9360
Fax: +45 8888 9394

Table of Contents

Introduction

The Struggle for the People is a short introduction to the modern history of Denmark. The read line is the transformation of the concept *people* from the time of the Reformation until today – with outlook to other European countries. The notion people is a dynamic concept. It is an idea that can take many shapes. The different shapes have to do with different perceptions of identity. To some extent the outbreak of new feelings of identity and new interpretations of the concept people has been the driving forces of changing the Danish society throughout centuries. In old Danish language, the notion people – in Danish *folk* – was for example not associated with a sovereign 'nation', but rather with 'household' and 'family'. In this sense the concept was always used in relation to a master. However, at a time *people* acquired a new meaning; it came to mean sovereignty and power, people's sovereignty and people's will. The transformation of the concept people: from being determined by its relation to a master to become its own master, changed the Danish society and made it modern.

In my work I am influenced by the linguistic turn – the crucial significance bestowed on language in the formation of the self and society. The disciplines of linguistics, narrative theory, and political theories concerning symbolic and imaginary aspects of politics have been an inspiration. Also Foucault's understanding of the individual as not only formed by different 'techniques of discipline' but also by an array of 'techniques of the self' has been applied in my work.

History is not only a matter of 'external' historical factors, but also a matter of 'internal' compositions concerning identity. The normative foundation of my work is based on the conception that history is a construction of the past. It is a matter of retrieving from the past the most beneficial points of reference wherein today we can glimpse ourselves. The way we construct the past has essential importance to the future. The future is dependent on a creative construction of the past, and is thus connected with a re-telling of history that can liberate forces hidden in other more outdated descriptions of reality.

This publication is mainly based on my book *Kampen om folket. Et dannelsesperspektiv på dansk historie gennem 500 år.* Gyldendal 2004. (*The Struggle for the People. Five hundred Years of Danish History Seen through an Educational Perspective*). In excess this publication also includes materials from two articles: Ove Korsgaard: "The Danish Way to Establish the Nation in the Hearts of the People". In John L. Campell, John A. Hall, and Ove Kaj Pedersen (Eds.): *National Identity and the Varieties of Capitalism.* The Danish Experience. McGill-Queen's University Press. Ove Korsgaard: "Giving the Spirit a National Form: From Rousseau's advise to Poland to Habermas' advise to the European Union". In *Educational Philosophy and Theory.* Vol. 38, nr. 2/2006. The publication also includes some materials from my contribution to the *Democracy Canon*, published by The Danish Ministry of Education 2008.

This publication is a follow-up on another pamphlet entitled *The Struggle for Enlightenment. Danish Adult Education during 500 years* and published 1998 by The Danish Chapter of the Association for World Education. The Danish AWE Chapter has also contributed to this publication. I appreciate and gratefully acknowledge this support.

Hopefully this publication can be a help to people who want to get a quick overview of Danish history throughout 500 years.

Ove Korsgaard
July 2008

Where Does the People Come From?

In this painting of the constitutional assembly, the two national liberal leaders D. G. Monrad and Orla Lehmann are placed as the dominating figures in the foreground. That was how the people behind the commission of the work wanted the historical event to be interpreted. However, the artist shows his sympathy for their opponent, N. F. S. Grundtvig, by placing him in the vanishing point of the picture.

Painting by Constantin Hansen, 1860-64. Det Nationalhistoriske Museum at Frederiksborg Slot.

What is the meaning of the notion *people*? Over time this concept has been interpreted in at least three different ways: *People* as a political entity (*demos*), *people* as a cultural entity (*ethnos*) and *people* as a social entity (*pléthos*).

In many discussions on democracy, the meaning of the term people or in Danish *folk* is often taken for granted. It is a prior assumption that the people was there before the emergence of democracy – that the people has been there since time immemorial. It is clear that the notion people was used before the invention of democracy and nation states, but the concept people was not associated with a sovereign people and a sovereign nation but rather with *household* and *family*. *People* in this sense was always part of a hierarchic structure that was determined by a relation between a master and a people. *People* understood as *subjects* was used in relation to the father of the house, the king of the country, as well as the lord God. During the period of absolute monarchy the words *people* and *folk* were used in particular as a designation for a social category; a distinction was drawn between 'upstairs' and 'downstairs', between master and servants, and the term was used when referring to the lowest levels of society – i.e. servants and subjects. Therefore, the discussion is likely to be more fruitful if we adopt the notion that the political meaning of the term *people* did not exist until a new meaning of the concept was introduced and gradually accepted.

Democracy presupposes a sovereign people; without the people, there is no rule by the people. Democracy – as an idea

– thus required a new interpretation of the word people. In his book *The social Contract* 1762 Rousseau (1712-1778) formulated the new principle: People as political sovereign. The decisive change came with the French Revolution when the term people was introduced as a concept in a new political structure. The result was a distinct change in the use of this word. However, the old notion of the concept did not disappear.

According to the Italian philosopher Giorgio Agamben (1942-): "Every interpretation of the political meaning of the term *people* must begin with the singular fact that in modern European languages, *people* also always indicates the poor, the disinherited, and the excluded. One term thus names both the constitutive political subject and the class that is, de facto if not de jure, excluded from politics" (Agamben 1995:176). In common speech as in political parlance, the Italien *popolo*, the French *peuple*, the Spanish *pueblo*, the English *people*, the German *Volk*, and the Danish *folk*, designate both the complex of citizens as a unitary political body and the member of the lower class. So what we called 'people' is in reality not a unitary subject but an oscillation between different poles. *People* is a contested concept placed between four opposite poles: up and down, out and in.

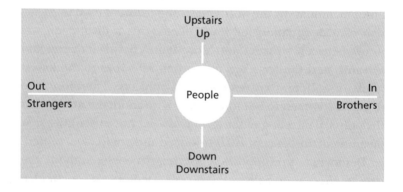

Not only the concept *people*, but also *nation* has changed over time. In Rome the concept nation was used to characterise strangers without Roman citizenship. In medieval time the concept nation was used at the new universities. For example, there were four nations in the University of Paris. The nation of France included all students coming from France, Italy, and Spain; that of 'Germanie', those from England and Germany; the Picard nation was reserved for the Dutch; and the Norman, for those from Scandinavia. It is important to note that the students had a national identity only in their status as students. However, the word nation came gradually to mean more than a community of origin: it referred now to the community of opinion and purpose. As universities sent representatives to adjudicate grave ecclesiastical questions to the Church Councils, the world underwent yet another transformation. Since the late thirteenth century, *nation* was applied to the parties of the ecclesiastical republic and acquired now the meaning of representatives of cultural and political authority. In the transition from the medieval time to early modernity, *nation* came to refer to the political, cultural and social elite. There were nations prior to the classic nation-state, namely nations of nobles. Starting in the late nineteenth century, however, these nations of nobles developed into nations of peoples. With this transformation, *nation* and *people*, referring to the top and the bottom of society, were merged (Greenfeld 1992:4f).

The American historian Liah Greenfeld points out that this merging occurred in England as early as the start of the sixteenth century and in the seventeenth century *Puritanism* appears to be at least as much a political term as a religious one (Greenfeld 1992:506). For example the English puritans declared in a manifest published on 4 January, 1649: "1) That the People are, under God, the original of all just Power. 2) That the Commons of England, in Parliament assembled, being chosen by and representing the People, have the supreme power in this nation" (Schuyler 1929:82).

On the continent, this did not happen until the French Revolution, which led to an enormous shift in the symbolic order of society. Where the king's throne represented divine power, the rostrum of the people became the symbol of the order of democracy. In the declaration of human rights, it is stated that all sovereignty comes from the nation – i.e. the nation and the demos are one. In article 3 of the declaration it is stated: "The principle of all sovereignty resides essentially in the nation. No body or individual may exercise any authority which does not proceed directly from the nation". The sovereignty of the absolute monarch rested on the notion that he personified God's order on earth. The sovereignty of the nation, by contrast, derives from human society. For the nation refers back to the people and its history. *Nation*, however, did not only come to mean a sovereign people but a unique sove-

Transformation of the idea of the nation

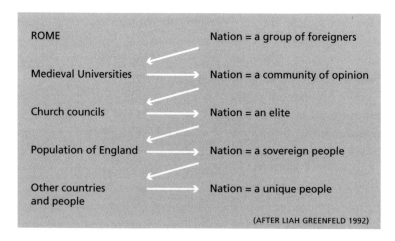

ROME   Nation = a group of foreigners

Medieval Universities   Nation = a community of opinion

Church councils   Nation = an elite

Population of England   Nation = a sovereign people

Other countries and people   Nation = a unique people

(AFTER LIAH GREENFELD 1992)

reign people, that is to say that *nation* is synonymous with *ethnos*. These two meanings express two different kinds of national identity and national consciousness and as well two kinds of collective units.

At a certain point in history, according to Liah Greenfeld (1954-), "the word 'nation' in its conciliar meaning of 'an elite' was applied to the population of the country and made synonymous with the word 'people'. *This semantic transformation signaled the emergence of the first nation in the world, in the sense in which the word is understood today, and launched the era of nationalism*" (Greenfeld 1992:6). (See figure p. 16).

In the following I will focus on the transformation of the concept people and look at its implications for the Danish state, the political system and the aim of education. An overview of five hundred years of Danish history is given in the following diagram.

1536-1776	1776-1849	1849/64-1945	1945-1989	1989-
Christian prince-state	Enlightened prince-state	Democratic nation-state	Democratic welfare state	Democratic member state
People as subject	People as subject	People as sovereign	People as sovereign	People as sovereign
Absolutism	Absolutism	Democracy	Democracy	Democracy
Protestantism	State patriotism	National language	National welfare	European values
Christian enlightenment	State enlightenment	Popular-national enlightenment	Popular personal enlightenment	European enlightenment
The shorter Catechism	Lives of Eminent Danes, Norwegians and Holsteinians	Danish literary history and The History of the Danish people	What is democracy?	?

I. Christian Prince-state

1536-1776

In 1529, Luther wrote *The Shorter Catechism*, which had an immense influence on general education and upbringing. This painting depicts an examination in *The Shorter Catechism* in the church of Hitterdal in Norway.

Painting from 1847. Dansk Skolemuseum. Reproduced with kind permission from: Korsgaard, Ove (2004): *Kampen om folket*. Gyldendal, Copenhagen.

A Christian Upbringing

Paternalism is the perpetual alternative to democracy. Either a master rules the people or the people rule themselves. You are in principle always subjugated to a master in a paternalistic state. Accordingly, the possibility of freedom is found 'outside' the walls of paternalism. Martin Luther (1483-1546) held a sincere belief in political paternalism, but turned against religious paternalism. People were, according to Luther, in two realms, one worldly and one spiritual.

Luther is the personification of the break with the medieval concept of a unified Christianity controlled by two swords – the swords of the pope and the emperor. In order to replace the two-sword-model, Luther developed his two-rule teaching, based on a distinction between the worldly and spiritual rule. The hard line Luther drew between the spiritual and the worldly is not – as often claimed – a strict separation of state and church, but merely between the state and the 'invisible' church. Following Augustine (354-430), Luther distinguishes between the visible and the invisible church. When you belong to the state, you are obliged to be a member of the visible church – the institution. Salvation, however, is not secured by a membership of the visible church. Faith is the foundation of salvation and faith is an existential matter. The visible church and the state are thus closely related in the two-rule teaching.

Luther considers reforming the universities as the key to the reformation of the church in general. Luther did not believe in theoretical truths removed from human existence. He was thus at odds with Aristotle – whose philosophy was of major importance to the medieval university. A considerable reduction of the Aristotelian influence on the universities was needed. The education and formation of the youth were to Luther of vital Christian interest. Society's ability to function was completely dependent on the quantity of qualified priests, civil servants, fathers and mothers. To Luther, the aim of upbringing and education was to prepare the individual to be a suitable citizen and upholder of the two kingdoms. Only in this way law and order could be upheld and peace endure. In 1529, Luther wrote *The Shorter Catechism* that contained the minimum of what the citizens should know about Christianity. *The Shorter Catechism* became the canon. Few books have enjoyed such a distribution or such an influence on general education and upbringing.

The history of the press and the growth of Protestantism are inextricably bound together. Gutenberg's (app.1397-1468) invention of the press was then what modern information technology is to society today. Luther considered this new technology a gift from God, and was very apt at using the new medium. Though the notion 'fundamentalism' is of a more recent date, the phenomenon can be traced back to the Reformation where the written word gained an unprecedented authority. With the Lutheran orthodoxy around 1600, 'true faith' as founded on the scripture was on the rise. This fundamentalist reading of the scripture had a major impact on the transformation of the worldview of the medieval time. Now there was another authority next to the authority of the church and the cultural norms of lineage and household.

Luther was in no way an advocate for a liberal society with religious tolerance and religious liberty, quite the contrary; he helped conjure up a powerful hostility. Religious liberty in the spiritual realm did not lead to religious liberty in the worldly realm. To Luther, the worldly realm was a Christian rule. Society's solidarity should be based on Christian religion, not on national culture. Failure to worship was a grave offence – a lesson that the Jews were taught in a very uncompromising way.

The Danish Prince-state

The Reformation fractured Christianity that brought about immense religious tension and opposition throughout Europe, accompanied by more than a hundred years of gruesome wars. A peace treaty between the Protestants and the Catholics was signed in Augsburg in 1555. The power of the princes was secured with the doctrine: *cujus regio, ejus religio* – the prince in power decides the religion. But the final breakthrough in the attempts to control the religious conflicts did not come about until the peace of Westphalia in 1648. The medieval time was not over until the peace of Westphalia in 1648 and a political system in place that could manage the changes brought about by the Reformation. The peace at Westphalia was a milestone in European history and determined the principle of the states' sovereignty within its own territory lasting up until World War II.

In Denmark, the relation between state and church was radically altered by the Reformation in 1536. The Reformation was not just a change of faith, but a change of rule too. The power of the king was strengthened and the power of the church weakened. The new state-judicial order meant that the bishops were stripped of their direct political power. This loss of political power was balanced by the increase in cultural influence as the church became the central institution of the state's enlightenment strategy.

The Reformation furthered a development of sovereignty, which in the long run became manifest in two different state systems in Europe – a parliamentarian and an absolutist system. While England ended up with a version of a representative system, absolutism gradually got the upper hand on the continent. Twelve years after the peace of Westphalia, Absolute Monarchy was instated in Denmark. The king became the sovereign power within the territory, at the same time a worldly authority and God's representative. The Reformation and the instating of Absolute Monarchy introduced social equality in two steps: First, the subjugation of the clergy in 1536 and second, the subjugation of the aristocracy in 1660. Absolute Monarchy was instated when the Danish territories of today's Sweden were lost to Sweden in 1558-60. It meant that Sweden broke Denmark's centuries old domination in Scandinavia.

The Identity Politics of the Prince-state

The legal system of the new church-government was instated by the so-called church ordinance 1537/39. The sermon came to be an essential part in the order of the new liturgy. The heart of the service shifted from the celebration of Mass to the sermon. Who were part of the congregation and thereby also member of the society was defined by access to the communion table. The communion became a condition for certain civil rights. The key to the priest's place of power lay in his administration of the sacraments: He decided who in the congregation was eligible for communion. Christian enlightenment was, by the time of the Reformation, a condition for joining the communion table. *The Shorter Catechism* was required reading. Like Luther, who translated the Bible into German, Chr. Pedersen (d.1554) translated it into Danish; and Hans Thomensen (1532-73) developed the psalm-strategy in Denmark as he attempted to get youths "to replace the papist songs and the despicable sexual chants" with 'decent' psalms

(Malling 1978:46). The reformers considered reading skills an important element in the struggle against the false doctrines. *The Shorter Catechism* was the people's access both to a world of faith and the written word, which, long before ordinary schools were established, helped to begin making the Scandinavian people literate.

Protestantism is not an unequivocal phenomenon. While Luther played a big role in the reformation of Germany and Scandinavia, the Protestantism that evolved in north-western Europe took an alternate course that was influenced by Jean Calvin (1509-1564). In Calvinism, Protestantism came to have a more systematic and ascetic form than was the case in Lutheranism. Asceticism was not seriously accepted until the appearance of Pietism in Denmark in the 1700's. Then it came to be a way of changing lifestyle and behaviour. Asceticism helped further a more productive way of life. The Pietistic enlightenment strategy was to interweave learning and emotion. In a matter of few years, a series of steps were taken by the state to strengthen Christianity as the heart of society. The most important were the confirmation ordinance in 1736, Pontoppidan's Catechism clarification in 1737 and the School decree in 1739. Even though the Pietistic school reforms suffered some setbacks, they were not given up but rather advanced with new strength by the turn of the century, albeit in a new and more rationalistic version.

Passing on the ideas of the Reformation to the people was the first major popular enlightenment undertaken and the state was its driving force. The content of these ideas was religiously coercive and socially normative. It is hard to imagine any other literature having as strong a grip on people's worldviews as the religious textbooks published after the Reformation had. The state-church doctrines were as omnipresent in the individual's daily life as the Koran is in some Muslim countries today.

II. Enlightened Prince-state
1776-1849

Two boys, two styles, the very same artist. The Danish painter Jens Juel painted a boy of the aristocracy in 1787 and a boy af the bourgeoisie in 1802. The French revolution in 1789 changed the views of the world. The running boy expresses the new ideals inspired by Rousseau and Kant. Gymnastics including running were part of an attempt to overthrow what they viewed as the aristocracy's decadent ideals.

To the left: Painting by Jens Juel, 1787. Photo: Danmarks Kunstbibliotek. Reproduced with kind permission from: Korsgaard, Ove (2004): *Kampen om folket*. Gyldendal, Copenhagen. To the right: Painting by Jens Juel, 1802. Statens Museum for Kunst.

From Christian Upbringing to National Formation

The Enlightenment was a new era in the histories of European ideas. But what is enlightenment? The German philosopher Immanuel Kant (1724-1803) answers the question in the following way in 1784: *"Enlightenment is man's emergence from his self-imposed immaturity.* Immaturity is the inability to use one's understanding without guidance from another. This immaturity is self-imposed when its cause lies not in lack of understanding, but in lack of resolve and courage to use it without guidance from another. Sapere Aude! Have courage to use your own understanding! – That is the motto of enlightenment" (Kant 1993:71).

According to thinkers of the Enlightenment the human being is nothing at the outset; the human being is 'formed'. *Bildung* was an essential word in German education and educational theory and became a key notion in an entire pedagogical philosophy. Even though there was no unified theory in educational thinking, there was nonetheless a theoretical basis that tied the strands together. This often overlooked basis is the individual's relation to itself, to society and to the world. This triple relation is the structural basis of what could be considered the trinity of general education theory. In regard to the individual's relation to society, however, immense theoretical differences appear. To Herder (1744-1803) and Fichte (1762-1814), the acquisition of language is considered a cornerstone of society, while Rousseau and Kant felt that the constitutional state and the social contract are at society's core. This difference led to two different meanings of the word *nation*, namely nation as ethnos and nation as demos.

While Rousseau created the connection between *nation* and *people* in France, Herder did the same in the German-speaking areas. They both regard general education and upbringing as the means to social changes, but disagree radically on several other crucial issues. While Rousseau refers to two metamorphoses and clearly distinguishes between the formation of the individual and the formation of society, Herder considers the

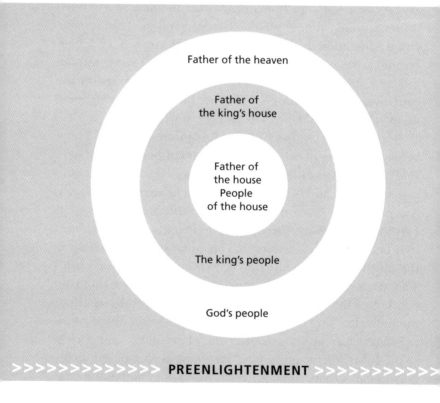

Father of the heaven

Father of
the king's house

Father of
the house
People
of the house

The king's people

God's people

>>>>>>>>>>>>> **PREENLIGHTENMENT** >>>>>>>>>>>>

two part of one and the same process. Rousseau singles out nature and art as the departure points of the individual's and society's formation respectively; Herder, on the other hand, regards organic nature as the ideal of both processes of formation. Unlike Herder, Rousseau does not regard society as an organic product but as an artificial product.

Though Kant and Fichte advocate the constitutional state and the ethnic nation-state respectively, they agree in wanting the young out of the homes. The influence of the mother and father in the home was considered as a hindrance to the modernisation of society. Kant's pedagogical philosophy can be un-

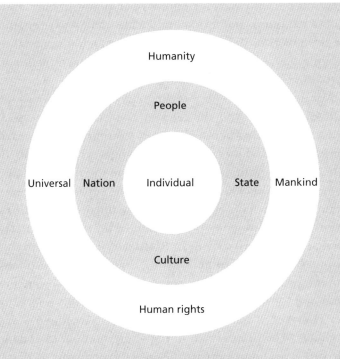

derstood as a radical break with the father as guardian. Kant hoped to separate the home and society in general, and the public school was seen as a new institution of vital importance. Kant advocates a public rather than a home-based education. He supported a cosmopolitan upbringing, and believed that a public school was needed (Kant 2000:29). Fichte was also concerned with liberating the youth and the children from the order of the household. It was literally a matter of isolating the young from the home. In his contribution to the groundwork of a new university in Berlin, Fichte points out that the studies necessitate "a complete separation of the student from every other form of life and absolute isolation." (Lyhne 2000:40). However, not only society's elite was supposed to have a new kind of education and formation: Fichte wanted to strengthen the formation of the German nation through a national upbringing, i.e. a common education for all citizens with complete disregard of social standing.

Not until the end of the eighteenth century did European philosophy break with the ancient conception of the social sphere as consisting of two elements, *oikos* and *polis; oikos* is the house (including production and economy), and *polis* the state. However, within modern capitalism the notion changed its meaning to include the characteristic separation between household and business that we know today. Instead of two sectors, house and state, society changed into three: The state, the market and civil society. In Rousseau's Encyclopaedia article on *Political Economy* he is saying that the word 'economy' can only properly be used to signify the fathers' government of the house for the common welfare of all, and this is its actual use. However, a new kind of economy is emerging, a state economy. "The primary aim of the entire household's labours is to preserve and to increase the father's patrimony, so that he might some day divide it among his children without impoverishing them; whereas the treasury's wealth is but a means, often poorly understood, of maintaining private persons in peace and plenty" (Rousseau 1997:4). To govern a state means to set up an economy at the level of the entire state, this means all its inhabitants, and the wealth and behaviour of each and all. Rousseau pointed to the problem that the word 'economy' essentially signifies the management of family property by the father, but that this model is becoming old fashioned. The new economy called political economy can not be reduced to the old model of the family.

From Guardian-rule to Democracy

Democracy was not introduced in Denmark at the end of the 18th century, but agricultural and educational reforms were introduced, inspired by the same ideas that constituted the foundation of the *American Declaration of Independence* of 1776 and the *French Declaration of the Rights of Man and the Citizen* of 1789. These are ideas as fellow citizenship, freedom of the press, the general public, civil society and personal freedom – all key ideas in a modern democracy.

In Denmark, the period from 1776 to 1848 can be considered a gradual transition from household to nation as the home of the people. A new national law of 15 January 1776 mentioned for the first time the citizens of the state – even though the term 'subject' did not disappear. With this law it was established that persons born inside the monarchy, with few exceptions, had the exclusive right to hold official office. However, the law served not only an exclusive, but also an inclusive purpose. It was meant to strengthen the cohesion of the so-called United Monarchy, which also included Norway and Holstein. This new status as citizen facilitated a development of an identity shared by countrymen irrespectively of the class structures of feudal society. The introduction of *citizen* heralds the coming of other concepts such as the *civil public* and *the civil society*.

Tyge Rothe (1731-1795), one of the key figures of the Danish Age of Enlightenment, struggled to hinder a nationalistic interpretation of the concepts *people* and *fatherland*. In an article: *Tanker om Kierlighed til Fædrelandet* (*Thoughts on Love of the Fatherland*) 1759 he underscored: "The people among whom a man lives as a citizen, they are his fatherland. I shall give the meaning of the word: Fatherland means the people and not the land on which they live. Fatherland means the people with whom we as citizens are united and not those among whom we first saw the light of day" (Rothe 1759). As a comment to the new law of 1776 he referred to nationality as a precious gift, but warned against the risk that exaggerated patriotism might lead to strife among the three large linguistic groups in the state. Rather than divide, nationality should contribute to uniting the people of Holstein, Norway and the Kingdom of Denmark in a community of citizens. The new status as national is clearly linked to the emergence of a new identity as a fellow citizen. Even if the law did not use this concept, the word fellow citizen was frequently used in odes and speeches on festive occasions, following in the wake of the introduction of nationality; for example Tyge Rothe addressed his audience with the word 'fellow citizen' in a speech to the Selskab for Borgerdyd (Society for Civic Virtue) 1785.

The emancipation of peasants was also an important element of the long-term strategy of absolute monarchy. According to a Regulation of 8 June 1787, the aim was "to abolish any sovereignty on the part of the landowners in relation to his copyhold tenants and make the entire relationship subject to general laws and rules". A regulation which followed in 1788 on the termination of adscription endowed the individual with a new civil status. The termination of the adscription was in fact primarily a military reform meant to do away with the household as the basis of the draft. Until then, the lord's house (or estate) was obliged to send soldiers to the army, but now it was the individual's duty to enlist. With the removal of the household as the basis for enlistment, the power of the lords over the peasants was weakened and the state strengthened.

The law was backed up by whole series of attempts to build a common patriotic feeling in the fatherland in general and for the king in particular. Examples of these ideological initiatives were the publication of a new canon called *Lives of Eminent Danes, Norwegians and Holsteinians,* written by Ove Malling, a 29-year old historian.

Educational reforms were specially initiated by the so-called philanthropists. They had a radical disagreement with the biblical understanding of man that has been central for educational thought in the European tradition from the medieval time to the coming of Pietism. Upbringing was to be motivated exclusively by 'worldly' matters. To some, the philanthropists were educational pioneers and others regarded them with distrust and resented them as revolutionaries. A newly established teacher training college, *Blaagaard Seminarium,* became a popular scapegoat. Some ecclesiastics were extremely sceptical towards the idea of educating an autonomous teaching corps that was not subjugated to the church. The authorities were worried as well, and started educating the teachers at designated rectories around the country.

In 1800 the philanthropist L.C. Sander (1756-1819) from Holstein was in appointed the first professor of pedagogy in Scandinavia. The brothers Christian Ditlev (1748-1827) and Ludvig Rewentlov (1751-1801) became the leading force in nearly all educational reforms in Denmark. The pedagogic reforms were a part of the United Monarchy's attempt to further the cosmopolitan conception of the fatherland. The Rewentlow-brother's school reforms had both an instrumental aim and an identity-political aim. The school was set up to give the peasant population useful skills and at the same time to fortify the state-patriotic conception that everyone, in spite of nationality and language, was a citizen in the United Monarchy.

The philanthropist invented gymnastics as an important part of the educational reforms. Gymnastics were a part of an attempt to overthrow the aristocracy's decadent ideals. Jens Juel's painting *The running boy* in front of *Christiani Institut* (a philanthropic school) expresses these new ideals. The English Garden was not created solely for physical growth, but also for spiritual maturation. Running became a sort of ascetic praxis characterised by Michel Foucault (1926-1984) as a technique of the self, a way for the individual to better oneself by the natural sentiments that has been woken. Gymnastics played a part in the self-discipline practice of the bourgeoisie as well as in the state's disciplining of the peasantry's young men, who were to acquire necessary military skills through common school and training school.

Not since the reform-period of 1789 to 1814 have so many educational reforms been implemented in Denmark in such a short time. The system introduced then was founded on three types of schools: The common school, the school of the bourgeoisie and the school of the learned (including the university). It was of crucial importance to the aristocrats, who had a stronger cosmopolitan view, that the nationalistic thoughts that were spreading within the market towns did not win foothold in the countryside. They had considerable success, and nationalistic thought among the peasants did not appear until the coming of democracy. Amongst the bourgeoisie, the civil servants and the artists, however, landlords did not succeed.

In 1808 Laurits Engelstoft (1774-1851), who became professor in history at the University of Copenhagen in 1803, published his principal work *Thoughts on National Upbringing* wherein he raised the question: What kind of upbringing is required to tie the societal body together? Engelstoft was the first to refer to language as the demarcating criteria of the nation, and has for that reason been called Denmark's first nationalist. But as he was devoted to the multinational United Monarchy, his political and cultural interpretation of the nation was strained to the breaking point.

In the first decades of the nineteenth century, the concepts nation and people gradually got a new meaning. Within literature, there is a shift from artistic poetry to national literature, and within history, a shift in focus from state history to national history. Herder was an important inspiration for this transformation. In Denmark, Henrik Steffen (1773-1845), who made some famous lectures in Copenhagen 1802-03, became another important catalyst for these new thoughts.

More than anyone the poet, clergyman and politician N.F.S. Grundtvig (1783-1872) was the spiritual mentor to those who had left the traditional community based on lineage and household to partake in the national body. Grundtvig grew up in a society whose worldview was characterised by Luther's thoughts on vocation and social standing. Lutheranism was not only the foundation of the church, but the moral foundation of the state as well. In becoming the leading advocate for the new view, Grundtvig helped revise the Lutheran basis insofar as it was not Christianity but people's language that was to be the moral basis of state and school. Thus, after 1825 Grundtvig criticised three fundamental Lutheran dogmas: the dogma of the scripture, the dogma of human nature as fundamentally sinful, and the dogma of the state. The church's alliance with the state since Constantine the Great was to Grundtvig nothing short of a fall of the church. That Grundtvig can be ascribed to so many opposing conceptions and opinions is due to the fact that he placed himself in the ideological crux of English liberalism and German nationalism. He was under a great influence from Herder and Fichte as well as English Liberalism's ideals of freedom. Grundtvig was convinced that freedom, as a shared cultural ideal, is a precondition for a true popular community. In the end, neither laws, rules nor institutions are capable of upholding freedom – only freedom can uphold freedom.

The transformation from a Christian Prince-state to a democratic nation-state necessitated a clarification of the relationship between religion, state and politics. What was the moral foundation of society if not Christianity? The apple of discord was the catechism teachings. Teacher Rasmus Sørensen (1799-1865) a leading lay preacher, wanted to continue the teaching of the catechism in the schools. Grundtvig wanted this abolished, arguing that only as a free endeavour could Christianity serve as a pillar for society. According to Grundtvig the mother tongue should replace Christianity as the moral foundation of the state.

The growing awareness that the mother tongue had fundamental importance to the national-political education placed the humanities in a crucial position within identity politics. By giving the humanities a more nationalistic content, they could help produce the kind of knowledge that was needed when building a nation. The institutional consequences of the nation building of the humanities can be observed in the configuration of the University of Copenhagen: From 1833 and throughout the century, a series of new professorships were established, the most important was a professorship in Danish language in 1844. The professors' production of knowledge was inextricably bound to the teachers' distribution of knowledge. The schoolteacher can thus be regarded as the professional general educator of the democratic nation-state.

New festivities helped facilitate the transformation from *commoners* to *people* as well. Newspapers were not widely distributed, and the censorship of many countries made it very difficult if not impossible to address political issues. Popular festivals were, considering the situation of the press, one way to reach a greater audience. The two popular festivals that had the greatest impact on the lingual politicization in Denmark took place at *Skamlingsbanken* in 1843 and 1844. The vigour and passion of the festivities were caused by an event that came to have enormous symbolic significance: Peter Hiort Lorenzen (1791-1845) spoke Danish instead of German in the assembly of the Estates of the Realm in Schleswig on 11 November 1842, an iconic event celebrated at *Skamlingsbanken* in 1843. In 1844, a new mass gathering took place; all the prominent Danish National Liberals from Copenhagen were present – including the historian and poet N.F.S. Grundtvig and the journalist and writer Meir Goldschmidt (1819-1887).

The popular festival was an inspiration to founding *Rødding Højskole* in 1844. The first principal of the school, Johann Wegener (1811-1883), figured prominently in the struggle for the promotion of the Danish language in Schleswig. An awakening of the farmers' sons – not politically but culturally – to the realisation of nationality was crucial in the language feud. It was the cultural integrity of the people rather than sovereignty of the people that was at the root of Johann Wegener's interpretation of the national.

In the United Monarchy the grand question from 1830 to 1864 was how it was possible to implement democracy while keeping the multinational United Monarchy together that was threatened by growing national controversies. The monarchy was still a multinational and multilingual composite of the

Kingdom of Denmark and the duchies Schleswig, Holstein, and Lauenburg; the north Atlantic isles – Iceland, Greenland and the Faroe Islands – and a few minor colonies around the world.

One problem of democracy is its need for a people, a *demos* – but what was the people of the monarchy? Were the people the entire population? Or could there be more than one people within the state? The answer depended on how *people* and *nation* were understood. Did *demos* disregard *ethnos*? Or was a *demos* actually dependent on a united *ethnos* and a people unified by a language?

The debate over the future of the monarchy was not only a matter of German versus Danish, but also a matter of local or central administration. While professor in philosophy F.C. Sibbern (1785-1872) advocated a federated state, the National Liberal leaders like Orla Lehmann (1810-1870) and D.G. Monrad (1811-1887) supported a centralised nation-state with Copenhagen as the centre. This controversy was of major importance to the future of the monarchy, for it could only survive within a federative model.

The debate did also address the question: What is the difference between belonging to 'the commoners' and belonging to 'the people'? People became a normative and reflexive category when Grundtvig wanted commoners to regard themselves not as *commoners*, but as *people*. *People* is thus not an empirical but a normative category. 'The people' does not exist in itself, a people requires self-awareness as a people (Grundtvig 1968:259).

As mentioned, in the pre-democratic social order, the notion people was simply a category for the subjects. The people were subjects to the master of the house, the lord of a manor, the 'father' of the country, or to God. The old definition is still at work in the dictionaries throughout the nineteenth century but loses ground to 'people' as citizen, 'people' as constituted by language and origin, and finally 'people' as a lower class. This development leads to a number of usages of *folk* slipping out of use; war-folk, court-folk, boat-folk, country-folk and harvest-folk. The same thing happens to a series of folk-words regarding class, people's payment, people's room, people's kitchen and people's table. During the same period two new types of folk-words appear that refer to the people in a political and a cultural sense. The political sense appears in words like people's sovereignty, the will of the people, the people's parliament, and a people's poll. The cultural sense comes out in words like folksong, folklore, folk-costume (national costume), folkdance, people's spirit and people's soul. The people as *demos* and *ethnos* did not exist until the transformation of the concept people – from subjects to sovereign.

PEOPLE AS SUBJECT

Folk as 'class'	**Folk as 'host'**
people's payment (folkeløn)	war-folk (krigsfolk)
people's room (folkestue)	boat-folk (bådsfolk)
people's kitchen (folkekøkken)	harvest-folk (høstfolk)
people's table (folkebord)	fire-folk (brandfolk)

PEOPLE AS SOVEREIGN

Folk as ethnos	**Folk as demos**
folksong (folkeviser)	the will of the people (folkevilje)
folk fairy tale (folkeeventyr)	people's sovereignty (folkesuverænitet)
folk-costume (folkedragt)	people's poll (folkeafstemning)
folkdance (folkedans)	people's parliament (folketing)

With democracy, however, the people became sovereign and could no longer be categorised as mere subjects. The origin of this change and transformation in the history of ideas can be traced back to Rousseau and Herder, who, in the 1760 and 1770's, wrote key texts on philosophy of education and politics. Rousseau was the first to formulate the groundbreaking idea that the people hold the political power. From Rousseau came the impulse to regard the people as the ultimate sovereign within a new kind of political and governmental structure. Herder also formulated a groundbreaking principle, the principle that people hold cultural power. With Herder the notion people also came to denote specific peoples, independent of political systems. At the core of Herder's 'cultural' interpretation of the notion people, is an understanding of collective identity as a deep-seated reality shaped by language and culture, the understanding of people as ethnic groups. Rousseau and Herder both broke with the old notion of the people as subjects; however, they put forth two separate versions of the people as sovereign. While Rousseau tied his conceptions of sovereignty to establishing a social contract, Herder linked his to the recognition of a language with common origin.

From United Monarchy to Nation-state

When the democratisation of the Danish state took place, nationalism gradually replaced religion as the core of European collective identity. The process of democratisation did not, however, bring about a gradual progression toward modernity. Rather, this process led to a radical destabilisation – in fact, a complete breakdown of the existing multinational and multilingual state. Only after this breakdown could the nation-state become the exemplary model for the modern Danish state.

The process of democratisation in Denmark is an exceptional illustration of the tension between collective identities, political systems, and state-form. In 1789, when democracy began to be implemented as a new political system in Europe, there was as yet no fully realised nation-state. As a consequence of the Napoleonic wars, the Danish-Norwegian union was dissolved in 1814 as Norway came under Swedish sovereignty. But the state, the so-called United Monarchy, was still a multinational and multilingual composite monarchy. The majority of the population in the kingdom spoke Danish, though in Holstein they spoke German, and in Schleswig half the population spoke Danish and the other half German.

The relationship between state-form and political system was, as mentioned, not clear when democracy knocked on the United Monarchy's door in the spring of 1848. As democracy could threaten the existing multinational state, a series of royalists opposed its implementation as a political system. There was a major difference of opinion among advocates of democracy as to the future of the state-form: The fundamental issue was whether democracy actually required a new state-form or whether the new political system could be incorporated into the old state-form. In other words: Does the *demos* require a state with only one dominating *ethnos*, or could there be one *demos* in a state consisting of competing *ethnos*? The advocates of democracy proposed three different state-forms.

A Federation:

What one could call cosmopolitan democrats proposed a free constitution within a federative configuration of the state and suggested Switzerland and North America as models. According to journalist and author Meir Goldschmidt, Denmark should – as Switzerland did in 1847 – create a "federation of states wherein the different nationalities are thriving and are ensured by the means of freedom" (Goldschmidt 1849:344). This vision was a 'rainbow-state' within which the different nations Holstein, Schleswig and the Kingdom could live in the same state under a common constitution.

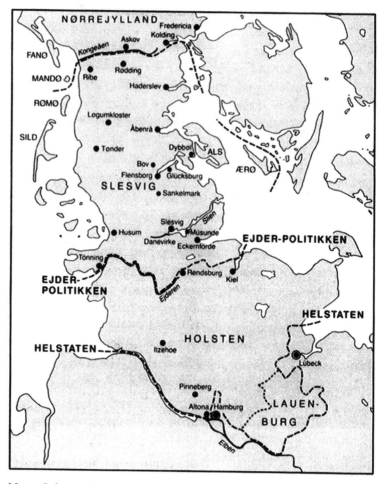

Map of the southern provinces of the United Monarchy, Sleswig and Holstein.

© Knud Rosenlund/billedkunst.dk. Reproduced with kind permission from: Korsgaard, Ove (2004): *Kampen om folket*. Gyldendal, Copenhagen.

The Eider-state:

The national liberals in Copenhagen fought for a free constitution within an Eider-state, which meant that Schleswig should
be included in the Kingdom and Holstein should be excluded.
The large German-speaking minority within the Danish state
was regarded as a threat to the future existence of the Danish
nation. It was feared that a fiercely expanding Germany would
use this minority as an excuse to turn against Denmark. History
later proved that this fear was well-founded.

Two States: Schleswig-Holstein and the Kingdom:

The national liberals in Kiel fought for a free constitution
within an autonomous state, which was to include Schleswig-
Holstein. Essentially, they demanded that Schleswig-Holstein
seceded from Denmark in order to be included as an autonomous state in the German confederation.

At the decisive meeting in the Casino Theatre on 20 March,
the national liberals in Copenhagen gained support for a
change of government in an Eider-Danish direction. The following day, 21 March, the national liberals organised a demon-
stration in which 15,000 men, led by the members of the City
Council of Copenhagen, approached the King with a demand
for a new democratic system of government. The demand was
backed up by the famous revolutionary threat: "We beg your
Majesty not to drive the nation to take desperate measures".

When the demand for democracy resulted in the fall of
absolute monarchy on 21 March 1848, disputes over the state-
forms surfaced. When the King stepped down as absolute monarch, a shift occurred in the symbolic order of power: from
royal sovereignty to popular sovereignty. This shift led to a
radicalisation of the controversial question that was already
being debated: Who are the people when the people are no

longer the King's people? There was considerable difference of opinion on this matter in the United Monarchy.

The proponents of democracy in the United Monarchy could not come together in one *demos*, and a civil war broke out. It was not a war played out between the proponents of the old and the new political systems, but a war among the various proponents of democracy. The first battle in this civil war took place near the small village Bov on 9 April 1848. The war ended in 1851 without solving the fundamental question: Who belong to 'the people' in the new democracy. Did the German-speaking population belong to a Danish demos? And did they want to belong?

The major powers in Europe would not allow changes to the borders that had been agreed upon in the *Congress of Vienna* 1814-15. The constitution that was instated on 5 June 1849 was considered radical, and the Eider-state was therefore connected with the democratic constitution in a way that was against the interest of Prussia, Austria, and Russia, where democratic voices were suppressed or never had got a foothold. The rulers of these countries did not find it desirable to have the constitution extended to Schleswig as well. This meant that the democracy instated in 1849 ended up applying only in the Kingdom (that is, to Kongeåen). The fact of the matter was that the United Monarchy ended up with two constitutions: one for the kingdom and one for the duchies.

From 1851 to 1864 the main question was still whether it was possible and desirable to implement democracy as a political system in a federation, in the Eider-state or in two states – the kingdom and Schleswig-holstein. In 1850 the lawyer and civil servant A.S. Ørsted (1778-1860) tried to reason with his fellow countrymen by warning them against new nationalistic movements in the kingdom as well as in the duchies. He published a historical and state-judicial writing, *For the sake of the*

Danish state's preservation in its entirety, in which he defended ethnic pluralism against the national liberals. In the introduction, he wrote: "The considerations, in regard to the relations between Denmark and the duchies Schleswig and Holstein, which I hereby put forth to my fellow countrymen, are so divergent from the conceptions, which, in stark internal conflict, by now have developed and finally achieved an almost absolute control, in one or the other part of the state's population, that there seems to be no prospect of them getting through" (Ørsted 1850:iii).

Ørsted knew that the odds of reasoning with the two parties, the Danes and the Schleswigholsteinians, had not improved with the events that had "caused dissension and finally civil war in our previously happy fatherland" (Ørsted 1850:iv). Indeed, they had done quite the opposite. Nonetheless, he made a final heroic attempt to avoid the dissolution of the United Monarchy by working out a plan for its preservation. He proposed a renewal of the monarchy "wherein all peoples, united by the Danish sceptre, ought to seek out their salvation." (Ørsted 1850:338). Ørsted considered the king to be the symbol of unity that was to bring the people together in one common state. This way of thinking, however, was in opposition to the demand for a free constitution with the people – rather than the king – in the symbolic centre. This turned out to be decisive. It appeared to be impossible to replace the king with the people as sovereign and at the same time keep the existing multinational and multilingual state together.

Not until the defeat by Prussia in 1864 and the resultant loss of Holstein, Schleswig, and Lauenburg did the 'solution' appear. With the loss of the duchies, Denmark came close to fulfilling the ideal requirements of a nation-state (i.e. a complete overlap of state, language, culture, and territory). There were, however, two elements that disturbed the idyllic image.

One of these elements was that the North Atlantic isles could not per se be regarded as part of the Danish nation-state. The other – and far more crucial – problem was that 200,000 Danes fell under German rule. The last matter did not get straightened out until the reorganization of Europe after World War I, which led to a plebiscite in Schleswig and the subsequent division of the old duchy. The northern half was incorporated into Denmark; the southern part remained German.

III. Democratic Nation-state

1849/64-1945

The introduction and development of democracy in Denmark is closely associated with certain social and cultural movements. The peasant and the folk high school movement and the labour movement have been the two most important movements behind the development in the Danish society from 1864 to 1972. The Danish painter Erik Henningsen (1855-1930) has portrayed Ludvig Schrøder speaking at Askov Folk High School as well as an agitator from the labour movement.

At the top: Painting by Erik Henningsen, 1902. Det Nationalhistoriske Museum at Frederiksborg Slot. At the bottom: Painting by Erik Henningsen, 1899. In a private collection. Reproduced with kind permission from: Korsgaard, Ove (2004): *Kampen om folket.* Gyldendal, Copenhagen.

The Ethnos-strategy

Why was it possible to establish a democratic federation in Switzerland and Belgium but not in Denmark? Why was a federal model not chosen in Denmark? As the Irish political scientist Brendan O'Leary points out, there are few good examples of the establishment of democratic federations that have been able to concurrently and successfully regulate the conflict between different ethnic communities. In successful cases, the communities have lived in relative segregation. "In Belgium, Canada and Switzerland the success of federalism in conflict-regulation, such as it is, had been based upon the historic accident that the relevant ethnic communities are quite sharply geographically segregated" (O'Leary 2001:50). In the United Monarchy of Denmark, there was actually a relatively clear-cut division between the German and the Danish-language communities that went right through the middle of Schleswig – approximately where the current border was drawn in 1920. This indicates that it would have been possible for the United Monarchy to become a democratic federation like Switzerland and Belgium.

The ethnically based nationalism played a major role in the creation of the Danish nation and was in part the reason that no federation was founded. The predominant view turned out to be that the borders of the *demos* and the *ethnos* should coincide.

This emphasis on language as the 'natural' foundation of socio-political unions had enormous political consequences for

Europe. The politicisation of language, which Herder founded but did not develop, shaped the political basis of the growing national groups in Europe by conferring major importance on all language communities. Poets, philologists, literati, and historians became the main champions in those 'language-battles' that broke out in Europe during the nineteenth century. Even though other weapons were in use, it was language itself that turned out to have the sharpest edge.

It is ironic – or tragic – that the concepts through which the linguistic or cultural nationalism were implemented in Denmark were developed by the 'enemy' – the Germans. And the more one depended on the German conceptualisation of 'nation' and 'national sentiment', the weaker the multinational United Monarchy became. The multilingual United Monarchy was weakened as a political entity with the politicisation of the language and the nationalisation of the culture. There were in Denmark – as in the multinational states of Austria and Switzerland – people who warned strongly against instating an ethnic principle of nationality as a state ideology. There was a successful balancing of the ethnic tensions in Switzerland and the Swiss confederation maintained a multinational state by clearly distinguishing *ethnos* and *demos*. There was not, however, a successful creation of a multinational state in Denmark or Austria. Though the Danish multinational state ultimately collapsed in 1864, the Republic of Austria did not break down until after World War I.

Seen in a power-political perspective, neither of the two major languages, Danish nor German, was strong enough to produce a linguistically homogeneous state such as France (Weber 1976). With only marginal domination, neither a policy of 'German-isation' nor one of 'Danish-isation' could fulfil the goal: one people, one language, and one state. Neither of them could obtain a hegemonic status within the existing multiethnic and multinational state. And when no accord on a federal state could be attained, the aforementioned civil war ensued in 1848–51 and then the war against Prussia and Austria in 1864.

There is a remarkable difference in the ways in which Denmark and Norway came to their democratic constitutions and were transformed into modern nation-states. In Norway the 1814 revolution was a double-revolution: An implementation of the constitution as well as national independence. While Norway turned 'modern' in one go, Denmark did it in three. First, the assembly of the Estates of the Realm in 1831–34; then the implementation of the democratic constitution in 1848–49, and finally, Denmark was transformed into an (almost) ethnically homogeneous nation-state from 1864.

The modern Danish nation-state was not formed by liberating itself from a larger political unit, as was the case with Norway, Belgium, Ireland, and Hungary. Neither did it unite hitherto separated territories the way state formation occurred in Germany and Italy. Rather, 'foreign' territories such as Norway, Holstein, and Schleswig were detached until the remaining part more or less corresponded to the ideals of the new nation-state – accordance of state, people, and language.

There were crucial differences in the processes of linguistic homogenisation in Norway and Denmark. In Norway the process was complicated by 'the era of the Danes', which by 1814 had lasted for 434 years. The question there was whether the new Norwegian nation-state should maintain the old written language, which it had held in common with Denmark for hundreds of years, or whether it should develop its own written language. Disagreement over the question resulted in an intense language feud that led to the formation of a new Norwegian written language alongside the old Danish written language (*bogmål*). One essential difference between the ways the debate about nationalism played out in Denmark and in Norway is that the Norwegian language-feud between *bogmål* and new-Norwegian was not interpreted as a conflict between two different *ethnic* groups, but rather as a feud between *social* groups – the 'upper class', who tried to maintain the old language of power, i.e. Danish, and 'the people', who wanted to speak their own 'original' language. In Denmark, however, the language-feud was represented as an ethnic issue. Even if the social question played an important role in the process toward democracy the feud was interpreted not only as a social struggle between the 'upper-class' and the 'people' but also as an ethnic-cultural struggle between Germans and Danes – between the 'people' and the 'foreigners' (Korsgaard 2004:304). This element was fatal to the United Monarchy's attempt to stay united.

What led to the defeat in 1864? This is one of the questions that has occupied Danish historians ever since. Among historians, there has previously been a strong tendency to focus on the military aspects of the matter, primarily the withdrawal from Dannevirke and the defeat at Dybbøl. But by focusing on the military aspects in the sequence of events, attention is drawn away from other aspects of identity-politics and cultural circumstances that also played a part in these events. The future of the state-form was actually not settled on the battlefield. It was settled by the particular sort of ethno-nationalism that emerged in Germany as well as in Denmark. While the army's withdrawal from Dannevirke must be considered a minor detail in the reshaping of the Danish state, the development of national tales and edification of a symbolic order must be ascribed vital significance. It was not the fight for Dybbøl that sealed the destiny of the United Monarchy; it was rather the figure of thought and the structures of sentiments that nationalism brought out (Korsgaard 2004:296–301).

Today, it is easy enough to deride the nationalists of those days. The crucial question is, however, whether the Danish state could have survived as an independent state in Europe had it not been for the Danish nationalists' demand for the state to be transformed into a modern nation-state. For not only was nationalism in fashion during the nineteenth century, but the nation-states' creation of an international state-system was underway as well. Nationalism was an integral part in the implementation of democracy, the establishment of nation-states and the development of modern industrialised states (Gellner 1994).

What we obviously cannot know is what would have happened in Denmark if Rousseau's social contract – political nationalism – had been ascribed more importance and Herder's language contract – cultural nationalism – less. We can never know if this would have led to the conservation of the multinational and multilingual state-form, or to the obliteration of the entire state: Jutland swallowed up by Germany and the isles united with Sweden. But however that may be, Denmark was, by the defeat in 1864, reduced to nothing but a small state in Europe.

Because the ethnically homogeneous nation-state has been regarded as the obvious framework of democracy since 1864, the question of whether a functional democracy within the framework of the United Monarchy could have been established has hardly been raised. An additional reason why this question has not been posed is related to the fact that nationalism, as a homogenising factor, relies not only on the ability to remember, but also on the ability to forget. After the war and in the wake of nationalism's advance, new stories and tales of what it had been like to be Danish in times past were developed and Denmark's past as a multinational state was soon forgotten.

Nationalism stages certain historical myths and allows others to slip out of our field of vision. Such a manoeuvre requires an active and conscious effort in a politics of remembrance. Danish historians began to tell the tale of the Danish state as a historical power that had existed since the dawn of time. But in order to establish and maintain such a way of recollecting history, it was necessary that historians partook in 'forgetting' and 'suppressing' certain events and processes related to the creation of the nation-state. To the Danes, it was about 'forgetting' how bloody the transition to democracy as political system and to the nation-state as state-form had been in Denmark (Korsgaard 2004:304–6).

The Decline of the Danish Mandarins

The introduction and development of democracy in Denmark is closely associated with certain social movements and philosophical currents. Democracy's introduction was in this respect promoted by the fact that the political, economic and cultural interests of the liberal middle class came into increasing conflict with the existing system that was characterised by the aristocracy's interests. The liberals demanded a constitution that gave citizens influence on political life and an economic policy that promoted freedom of competition.

It was the national liberal movement in Copenhagen that was the driving force behind the introduction of democracy in Denmark. Culturally, the national liberals – also known as the intellectuals' party – belonged to the educated middle class, who primarily comprised civil servants, lawyers, doctors, clergymen, newspaper editors and university academics. Their approaches to democracy were a top-down perspective. Roughly speaking, the majority of the people had to choose their leaders among a minority belonging to the (new) elite.

It is common in political theory to distinguish between political nationalism and cultural nationalism. But in order to describe how the nation was built in Denmark, we need to make a further distinction between state-nationalism and popular-nationalism – a distinction between top-down and bottom-up nationalism. The state and the civil society constitute the symbolic centres of the two kinds of nationalism, and these two centres are a part of all national and democratic movements. However, in certain national movements the state is regarded as the most important factor, while in others it is civil society.

As mentioned, German language and cultural-nationalism sped up the collapse of the United Monarchy. It is, however, surprising that Danish nationalism after 1864 came to differ quite radically from German nationalism. There are multiple explanations as to why the same kind of nationalism developed differently in the two countries. One is that state-nationalism in Denmark was seriously weakened by the defeat in 1864, whereas the nationalism of the populace was strengthened. This is connected with the different roles played by the academic elite in Denmark and in Germany. While the academic elite in Denmark lost its political and cultural legitimacy after 1864, it was the academic elite who helped establish the legitimacy of the new German nation-state.

As the American historian Fritz K. Ringer (1931-) documents in his classic book *The Decline of the German Mandarins* (1969), the 'mandarins' in Germany constituted a significant ideological factor in the development of the German nation-state. By 'mandarins' Ringer is referring to the bourgeoisie of higher civil servants (priests, lawyers, professors, and doctors) that appeared in the nineteenth century. This academic elite based its authority on cultural knowledge rather than on aristocratic traditions or economic and political power. To the mandarins, *Bildung* became a key notion; it was related to 'culture' and to internal cultivation rather than to 'civilisation', with its origins in rationalism's focus on utility. As the holder and administrator of a German *Geist*, the academic elite came to be very important to the legitimacy of the German state.

In the attempt to implement democracy and create an Eider-state, the Danish national liberals eventually won great cultural importance as well. When the sovereign king abdicated his throne on 21 March 1848, a new partly national-liberal government was formed. D.G. Monrad, the government's 'strong man', became the first Minister of Cultural Affairs. Next day, he had taken charge of the newly established Ministry of Education and Ecclesiastical Affairs. Monrad regarded the new ministry as a ministry of nation building. His plan was to create a ministry that administered everything related to "the creation of the nation and the spiritual interests of the state in general" (Petersen 1984:16). From the initial steps of democracy, he emphasised that his Ministry should be involved in everything that could further the creation of the state, and this applied in particular to the field of education. He wanted to separate school and church and to unify the institution of education. It is often overlooked that when Denmark became democratic there were two separate schools, the school of the common people and the school of the learned. The two institutions had each their own language of education. While Latin was used by the learned, Danish was the language in the school of the common people. To Monrad, it was crucial to the construction of the nation-state that the difference between the two educational institutions was bridged. "For the department of education might well contain different sorts of schools but these do, however, collectively constitute a unity wherein they together create a chain of institutions whose individual joints interconnect and support each other" (Petersen 1984:16).

In this passage, Monrad actually formulates the ideological foundation of the national common school (*enhedsskole*). However, more than fifty years had to pass before this ideology acquired structural and institutional consequences, and more than 100 years before the union school was fully realised.

Because Monrad was head of the government during the war with Prussia, and therefore particularly associated with the catastrophe, his power was broken in 1864. After the defeat, broken down by sorrow and an apocalyptic anxiety, he immigrated to New Zealand. But it was not only Monrad who was struck; the entire political elite of national liberals and thus the related cultural elite were crushed as well. When the Prussian soldiers stormed Dybbøl on 18 April, the political power of the national liberals came to an end. In the parliament, national liberals did not play a role in working out the revision of the constitution that was necessitated by the break down of the United Monarchy. Even though the national liberals rightly considered the 1849 constitution of their making, they were left with no influence when some representatives from the peasant class joined the landowners in making the so-called revised constitution of 1866.

The defeat of the national liberals became a determining factor in the development of the Danish nation-state. The defeat caused a new social group, namely the peasants and their cultural shock troops – the so-called Grundtvigians – to influence this development to a degree unparalleled in the rest of Europe. In the power-vacuum that appeared in the wake of the fall of the national liberals, the Grundtvigianism of the populace was the only movement with a fairly broad appeal. The workers' movement only appeared in 1871. It was thus not the national liberals but the Grundtvigians who came to influence the establishment of the state up until the workers' movement began to take over after World War I.

After 1864 greater attention was paid to Grundtvig's constant call to the people for active involvement, and far greater sympathy felt for his powerful critique of the Danish mandarins' educational program, characterized by state-paternalistic ideas. In the parliament Grundtvig fought to promote a liberal society; he would by that same token phase out a series of state institutions. He proposed abolishing the military draft, and making participation in defence voluntary. He was also an advocate for the highest possible economic independence and a spokesman for the abolishment of all coercive guild systems. Freedom of choice in regard to churches and schools was of particular importance to him, and he opposed all kinds of coercion when it came to schools and education.

The Danish mandarins kept on trying to assert themselves after 1864. On the initiative of the heads of the national liberals, the Committee for Advancement of the Enlightenment of the People was founded in 1866. National liberals saw a dire need for such a committee: "Our common people, the countryside people in particular, have yet appropriated so little of the middle-class' culture and spiritual interests." The common people in particular had not really acquired an awareness of their nationality. Thus, the main task was to enlighten the people so "that the social life and the state life can be saturated by the national spirit and consciousness" (Steenstrup 1865).

In 1870 the national liberal professor H.N. Clausen (1793-1877) all but implored from the podium at the University of Copenhagen for the Danish people to conform to the enlightenment that emanated from the university. "I cannot descend from this podium, whose engraving says 'in spirit and in truth' without pleading to our people: that it must become more and more worthy of help from above, more and more able to use the help, when the time of help is at hand" (Clausen 1870:14).

In short, with the guidance of the Danish mandarins, the rest of the population should partake in academic enlightenment.

But the Danish mandarins' plea to be heard was violently swept aside by Grundtvig. In his last speech at Marielyst Højskole on 2 November 1871, less than a year before his death at 89, the always ready-for-revolt Grundtvig rejected, with an edge-of-hand blow, the thought that his own notions of cultivation were meant to bridge the gap between the learned and the people. Such a prospect, according to Grundtvig, was a great misunderstanding. In order to lead to human enlightenment and cultivation it must: "emanate from the people itself, [because] the so-called academic enlightenment and cultivation that emanates from the foreign ... never reaches the people as living words, nor does any good for the fatherland, but leaves the people dumb and spiritually defenceless to be ridiculed by foreigners" (Grundtvig 1965:108).

The Rise of the Grundtvigian Movement

Whenever democracy is instated it is a delicate issue: Is it the state that, in order to secure national integration, should be responsible for all education, or should the state forego this responsibility so as not to undermine an important principle in democracy: the individual's autonomy? In other words, can the parents' right to direct their children's education be inferred from the fundamental democratic ideal of individual autonomy?

As the Grundtvigian movement advanced, the 'popular' became a counterpoint to the state. Grundtvigians challenged the state educational system (the common school, the Latin school, and the university), hoping to create an alternative, more 'popular', system with private schools (for children) and folk high schools (for young adults). The Danish mandarins' enlightenment, coming from 'above', was to a large extent accompanied by the Grundtvigian enlightenment coming from 'below'. The Grundtvigians succeeded in establishing a private school system alongside the public system.

After 1864 the Grundtvigians projected an impressive self-awareness. If we turn to the 85-year-old parish official Hans Christensen (1781-1868), we find a good example of the opposition to the Danish mandarins. In 1865, he made the following proclamation in regard to the private school in Vejstrup, Fyn: "I expect these schools to provide a great deal of good for the Danish people." He was hoping that a private school would be founded in every town, "so that the other little hells [i.e., the public schools] will be left empty." Adding to that he said: "And if we look at it politically, it is then in actuality the greatest of stupidities to think that state officials can educate a people to be free" (Markussen 1988:330).

The Danish mandarins and the Grundtvigians disagreed on the role of the state in the new ordering of society. Although they were in agreement in wanting to break with the strong position of the absolute monarch, they were in stark disagreement as to how radical that break should be. According to D.G. Monrad, the state had the authority to speak on behalf of the people, and could by that authority intervene and regulate social behaviour. The invisible hand of liberalism cannot alone be about society as 'a good community'; it takes the control of politics' visible hand and the 'morality' of society's institutions. To Monrad, the institutions of society were the corporal aspect of the community's ethical norms. To Grundtvig and the Grundtvigians, it was not the state institutions but the 'free' institutions that, ethically speaking, were the corporal aspects of the national community's norms.

It was, as we know, the Danish mandarins who began to reshape the state institutions of the absolute monarchy into democratic institutions. It was Monrad, for example, who, during the making of the constitution, formulated the notion of the people's church – *Folkekirken*. Later, the common school was renamed the people's school, the common library the people's library, and so on. But to many of the Grundtvigians it was not enough to change old state institutions into people's institutions; rather, new people's institutions had to be founded, as for instance 'open' or 'free' schools, 'free' congregations, and 'free' associations. According to Grundtvigianism, the public school could not, due to its ties to the state, be regarded as truly 'popular'. Only the 'free' school could be popular. By virtue of their liberal connotations, the notion of the 'popular' had become almost synonymous with what was outside the state. And in this manner, the notion of 'popular' in Denmark came to be equivalent with the liberal notion of voluntariness.

To be 'free' or 'open' – as an individual, an association, a school or a church was to Grundtvigianism, as well as to liberalism, to be free from the power of the state. In order to maintain such freedom, it was vital that the people be willing to make an effort voluntarily. Freedom and the volunteer-spirit are, in both traditions, two sides of the same matter. Freedom cannot ultimately be guaranteed by the state; only the people can secure freedom. And that can happen only with a foundation in 'popular' and 'civil' society. Open associations were seen as a sign of a voluntary social solidarity, which in turn was seen as the ideal for a grander popular and national society. Willingness to render voluntary and unpaid assistance was thus regarded as the ultimate test of one's civil virtues. Neither the state nor the free market could guarantee national solidarity; that depended on whether or not 'popular' and 'civil' society made up the moral foundation of society in general. According to the ideology of Grundtvigians one should manage without help from the state.

The educational politics of the Danish mandarins and the Grundtvigians who mainly spoke on behalf of the Danish farmers were in agreement having an obviously national point of departure, but they differed as to their views on the state and the people. While the bourgeoisie continuously bestowed essential significance on the state institutions, in the building of the nation, the Grundtvigians relied more on institutions outside the state. The national liberals and the Grundtvigians wanted to build the nation by means of a state-nationalism and a popular-nationalism, respectively.

Even though the Danish mandarins retained considerable influence throughout the century, the connection between political power and the academic elite was broken by the events leading up to the national catastrophe in 1864. It was of great significance for the development in Denmark that power shifted from the state-oriented academics to the non-state-oriented Grundtvigians. This meant that the Danish version of culture-nationalism diverged from the German, which had been the common background of both the Danish mandarins and the Grundtvigians. In Denmark, popular-nationalism contributed to the democratisation from 'below' and popular-education contributed to the formation of the nation in the hearts of the Danish people (Korsgaard 2004:342–7).

According to the Danish historian Uffe Østergaard, Grundtvig "produced a refined definition of national identity which set the tone for a nationalism less chauvinistic than most in the nineteenth century" (Østergaard 2006:76). In 1848, after the outbreak of the civil war over Schleswig, he wrote a song asking the difficult and controversial question: "What is a People?"

> People! What is a people? What does popular mean?
> Is it the nose or the mouth that gives it away?

Is there a people hidden from the average eye
in burial hills and behind bushes,
in every body, big and bony?
They belong to a people who think they do,
those who can hear the Mother tongue,
those who love the Fatherland.
The rest are separated from the people,
expel themselves, do not belong.
(Østergaard 2006:77).

What Grundtvig expressed in this verse has since become a standard formulation in Denmark of an anti-essentialist definition of national identity.

The Free-School as a Popular Institution

In 1850 Christen Kold (1816-1870), who must be acknowledged as the spiritual and pedagogic father of free schools, wrote a dissertation entitled *On the Children's School*. In the dissertation he argued that along with public education there should be private education, where "every man is allowed to care for his children's education as he sees fit, in so far as he can provide evidence that they do not lack education and progress compared to the children who are taught in the public school." (Skovrup, 1944:59). In 1852, Kold founded a free school in Ryslinge and the same year supporters of Grundtvig and Kold insisted on an act that would guarantee parents' rights to determine their children's education. In 1855, after three years of negotiating, the Free School Act was passed by parliament. Parents were now allowed to found their own schools, pay the costs and also appoint the staff. By passing the Free School Act, parents were no longer obligated to send their children to school; they were merely obligated to care for their education. The reason why National Liberals, like D.G. Monrad and J.N. Madvig (1804-1886), ended up voting for the Free School Act of 1855 was due to a higher set of standards regarding the content of the education in private schools. It was stated that the education in private schools had to be on a par with the levels in public schools (Korsgaard, 2004:333-37).

There are several reasons as to why the Grundtvigians began to establish free schools. Ultimately, however, the reason was that it would provide the elementary school with a new national content other than the old religious content. This caused a shift in the socio-ethical basis of the school, a shift from a Lutheran institution to a national institution. Among the changes was the replacement of Catechism teaching with lessons in national history and literature. However, in elementary school, which was rooted in the United Monarchy's ideology of state church and state patriotism, the changes would not come as quickly as the Grundtvigians demanded. The Grundtvigian free schools were not schools of the elite, and thus can not be considered to be akin to the English tradition of elitist private schools.

The Grundtvigians did not only establish free schools for children, but also boarding schools for young adults, called folk high schools. Already before 1864, the Grundtvigians had begun to establish folk high schools, but it was not until after 'the great disaster' in 1864 that the creation of these types of schools gathered proper momentum. Between 1864 and 1872, around 50 folk high schools were established, the vast majority of which were based on a Grundtvigian educational philosophy. In the Grundtvigian self-knowledge, freedom could not be guaranteed by the state, but by the people.

Not only did the Grundtvigian Cultural Revolution have a tremendous impact on the growth of civil society, but it affected the Danish capitalist market economy as well. The internationalisation of the 1870's – the first step toward globalisation – meant radically increased agricultural competition. Cheap grain, predominantly from the United States, gained a footing in European markets. New railroads and steamboats were the technological precondition that gradually made it possible to transport American grain to Europe while still keeping prices competitive. The growing crisis in Danish farming brought a demand for customs regulations; however, the call for protectionist policies never really caught on, and instead the agricultural industry responded to the crisis by shifting from grain to livestock production. This shift called for educational research and reforms of existing farming education, the establishment of a new agribusiness (i.e. the processing industry: dairies and slaughterhouses), as well as the setting up of a new distribution network. A key concern was whether 'agribusinesses' should be governed by the laws of capitalism – as the urban industries had been – or whether they should be based on ideas of co-operation. The Danish farmers' prevailing choice was to organise agribusiness and its distribution network as co-operative companies. In the eighteen-year period from the founding of the first co-operative dairy in 1882 to 1900, no fewer that 1066 co-operative dairies were founded, as well as a considerable number of co-operative slaughterhouses. Danish agricultural products were soon thereafter considered the finest in the steadily growing British market. The developing agriculture powered general Danish industrialisation up until the 1960's, and not until 1963 did industrial exports exceeded agricultural exports.

The way out of the agricultural crisis in the last decades of the nineteenth century has been a 'grand narrative' in Danish written history. This has often been a story about a close connection between cultural and material revolution – the Grundtvigian Cultural Revolution and its material consequences. The folk high schools regarded as an institution of formation as well as an educational body – not only skill training, but also creating national citizens – produced mental and cultural conditions that greatly contributed to the Danish peasantry's choice of the co-operative model (Korsgaard 1997:191–208). The story of the Danish folk high schools and the co-operative movement earned international renown in the twentieth century and inspired a series of reform movements in Eastern Europe in the inter-war period and in the Third World in the decades succeeding World War II.

How to Live with a Big and Strong Neighbour?

The war of 1864 was a turning point in Danish history, and led to a fundamental change in political thinking, as it had been expressed in Danish culture through literature and art, in historiography, and the overall enlightenment. The Danes' perception of themselves and the rest of the world were entirely altered.

The war was a turning point in German history too. With the war against Denmark in 1864, Germany, under the leadership of Bismarck (1815-1898), started on a road of expansionist politics attacking Austria in 1866 and France in 1870–71. These three wars altered the geopolitical situation in Europe and put Denmark in the following dilemma: Should the country be defended to the last man standing, or was Denmark to surrender the moment it was attacked by a major power? It was an extremely sensitive question. The majority of the population regarded Germany as the enemy, but it was nevertheless a hard geopolitical fact that Denmark, with its two million inhabitants, at this point was a neighbour of Europe's – and therefore the worlds – strongest power. In the days following 1864, Danish military policy was based on the possible scenario of retrieving Schleswig by joining a major European power in a war on Germany. This scenario had already broken down in France's defeat in the war against Germany (1870–71). From then on, it was no longer a matter of whether Denmark should join a war in order to retrieve Schleswig, but rather whether Denmark could protect its sovereignty by military means at all. If this was not possible, could sovereignty be defended by other means? The ensuing debate came to have a considerable focus on defence priorities: Was it the nation or the state that should be defended? Should state security be based on military power? Or, should the future of the nation be grounded in the hearts of the people?

Rousseau's *Considerations on the Government of Poland* (1772) may indirectly shed some light on the Danish situation. With Russia, Austria and Prussia as neighbours, Poland was surrounded by states with superior military capacity: "She has no strongholds to stop their incursions. Her depopulation makes her almost entirely defenceless" (Rousseau 1991:167). What is Rousseau's advice to the Poles? Mainly, it is to ground the Polish republic in the hearts of the Polish people. "I can see only one way to give her the stability she lacks ... it is to establish the Republic so firmly in the hearts of the Poles that she will maintain her existence there in spite of all the efforts of her oppressors" (Rousseau 1991:167–8).

In addition, Rousseau advised the Poles on how to sow the republic in the hearts of the Polish people. It could only happen through a national system of education that fortified the country by engendering patriotism: "It is education that must give souls a national formation, and direct their opinions and tastes in such a way that they will be patriotic by inclination, by passion, by necessity" (Rousseau 1991:172). Poland needed a new type of defence as well: "Poland is surrounded by warlike powers which constantly maintain large standing armies which she herself could never match without soon exhausting herself" (Rousseau 1991:182). It was impossible in the foreseeable future for Poland to defend herself by means of an expensive, ready army, said Rousseau; however: "You will soon, or more accurately speaking, you already have the power of self-preservation, which will guarantee you, even though subjected, against destruction, and will preserve your government and your liberty in its one true sanctuary, the heart of the Polish people" (Rousseau 1991:183). Rousseau suggested arming the people in the Swiss model: "Why not, then, instead of regular troops, a hundred times more burdensome than useful to any people uninterested in conquests, establish a genuine militia in Poland exactly as in Switzerland, where every inhabitant is a soldier, but only when necessary?" (Rousseau 1991:185).

A hundred years later, in a debate over Danish defence, a part of the left-wing put forward a number of viewpoints similar to those found in Rousseau's *Considerations on the Government of Poland*. While the right-wing proposed a standing army as the key element in the country's defence, the left wing advocated a defence based on arming the people. Grundtvig had already vehemently opposed the idea of a standing army in 1848, because he saw it as suppressing the peasant class. Therefore, as Rousseau had advised the Poles, so Grundtvig recommended the Danes: "Men of Denmark, as truly as we all constitute a freeborn royal people; no ordinary military service of bondage, but an arming of the people in freedom" (Grundtvig 1909:174). And in the defence commission of 1866, nearly all of Balthazar Christensen's (1802-1882) many contributions defended the idea of a 'people's army', a 'national guard', or an 'arming of the people'. To the left-wing it was a matter of securing the people's autonomy even in matters of national defence (Nielsen 1979:77).

The two predominant positions in the Danish defence de-

bate were: a standing army in combination with a strong forti-
fication of Copenhagen, or an arming of the people. There
was, however, a third proposal, whose foremost spokesmen
were the journalist and politician Viggo Hørup (1841-1902)
and the historian and politician Peter Munch (1870-1948).

The Liberal Party and the Social Liberal Party

One constitutional issue characterised the political dispute
from 1864 to 1901: should it be the king or the parliament who
appoints the government? Similar debates occurred in other
European countries, but in few places was the debate as long
and unyielding as in Denmark. The reason is mainly that the
fall of the national liberals brought the conservative landowners back into government. In Norway, conversely, the Liberal
Party (Venstre) took hold of government in 1884 and thereby
gained control of the state apparatus. The same did not happen in Denmark, even through Denmark's Liberal Party (Venstre) got a clear majority in the parliamentary election of 1884
as well.

In spite of great internal disagreement, the leaders of the
Left, Christian Berg (1829-1891) and Viggo Hørup, joined in
the vehement fight for cabinet responsibility in opposition to
the Estrup-government. The strategy of the Left was to weave
an unbreakable strand between the 'popular' and the notion
of democracy; this strategy was opposed by the Right's strategy
of separating the two.

In the last three decades of the nineteenth century, nationalism underwent a fundamental transformation in a number of
European countries. The Right adopted nationalism as an ideology and used it in the struggle with the Left, who had developed the ideology in their fight against the bastions of Conser-
vatism. The issue of national security proved to be an issue the

Right could use in the race for popular support. The shift from liberal to conservative nationalism can be summarised as a shift towards 'provincial' nationalism, a distancing from the city, urbanisation and industrialisation, and identification with nature, the village and the local society. It was difficult to reconcile this provincial nationalism with the nationalism that grew from the French Revolution and the American Declaration of Independence. This proved especially fatal in Germany that unlike Denmark, had not yet developed a democratic tradition to counter the new form of nationalism.

The election to the Folketing in Denmark on 3 April 1901 was epoch-making, in that the Liberal Party's (Venstre) demand for parliamentarianism was finally heard. However, in the first decades this was only as a fragile practice and not as a constitutionalised principle. The way was now paved for the first left-wing government, whose undisputed leader, J.C. Christensen (1856-1930), was first nominated Minister of Cultural Affairs and not Prime Minister. J.C. Christensen was the incarnation of the new self-aware class of teachers educated in teachers' colleges instead of the university. Even though the teaching profession during the 19th century had made its way up from the bottom to the top of the social pyramid, appointing a teacher from Jutland Prime Minister was too much of a break with accustomed thinking.

J.C. Christiansens goal as Minister of Cultural Affairs was to alter and democratise the ecclesiastic and educational systems so that these old bastions of general education came to reflect the popular revolution that, on the political level, had resulted in cabinet responsibility. The implementation of the intermediate school in 1903 and the parochial church counsel the same year were his main achievements. Not everyone on the left was pleased with J.C. Christensen's strategy of popularising the school and the church. Several prominent Grundtvigians were convinced that private independent schools were the ultimate token of popular self-organisation. Furthermore, numerous priests and bishops were furious because of his efforts to democratise the organisation of the church.

However, J.C. Christensen could not keep the Liberal Party together. Because of disagreements about the defence strategy in 1905, a fraction led by Peter Munch left the party and founded a social liberal party called *The Radical Left*. As a young historian, Munch had begun to develop a new defence strategy in the 1890's. The fundamental question was: How can a small country maintain its sovereignty in a world dominated by large ones? Munch's analysis of the international scene told him that the disproportion between Denmark's and Germany's military power had, since the 1864 defeat, become impossible to overcome: "Denmark, in any battle it could possibly end up in, will be pitched against such an overwhelming superiority that no matter how great the enthusiasm, it cannot lead to anything but more peril, more bloodshed and more destruction before the already given defeat" (Højrup 2002:333).

This perspective implies that military defence was hopeless: "If the Danish people built their future on military defence it would not build on the foundation of reality, but on the most fragile of illusions." To Munch neutrality was the only possible way for Denmark to preserve itself. However, neutrality alone would not be enough. The sovereignty of the country must still be defended but with means other than military. The sovereignty must be defended by establishing a society and a culture that make it possible to survive as a people even if the territory is occupied for a while. Here Munch drew on Poland as an example; even though the Polish state had been conquered a hundred years earlier (Poland was split between Russia, Prussia, and Austria in 1795), the Polish nationality was, according to Munch, "stronger today than it had been a hundred years ago." And went on to predict: "It is not impossible that Poland, yet again, can partake in world history" (Højrup 2002:333). In Denmark, it was fundamental to avoid creating the illusion that the country could be defended by the military: "And truly, it is of no misfortune to the people that they cannot sustain the creation of such a belief in defence. It is a quite unfounded and unsound claim that believing one can defend oneself is a vital-necessity for a people, a precondition for it to maintain its vitality and liveliness" (Højrup 2002:334). The lack of capacity to defend the country militarily must, according to Munch, be met with a will to form a society that the population appreciates; that is to say, with a national project that the people can be proud of and identify with.

This viewpoint on the future of Denmark became the basis of the party platform of the Social Liberal Party *(Det Radikale Venstre)*, in the so-called *Odenseprogram* of 1905. The *Odenseprogram* was prefaced with the statement: "Denmark declares itself continuously neutral." Then five main points laid the foundation of the society and culture that were to replace the military defence of the state. Munch's policies were: To defend the country by arranging the foreign and military politics according to the will of the major neighbour and, as an alternative to conventional defence, to build a strong internal defence primarily through social, educational, and cultural politics. What could not be known in 1905 was that the *Odenseprogram* formulated what later came to be the basic principle of the welfare state, which was established in the twentieth century. The main founders of this state-form were the Social Democrats *(Social-demokratiet)*, but it took place in close co-operation with the Social Liberal Party.

Socialism through Dictatorship or Democracy?

In 1848, Karl Marx (1818-1883) and Friedrich Engels (1820-1895) published *The Communist Manifesto*, which had the rallying call "Proletarians of all countries, unite!" The vision of united workers across national borders raised the question: How should a socialist relate to the question of nation and democracy? Could the principles of liberal democracy be maintained amidst efforts to realise a socialist society?

In the Versailles peace conference in 1919-1920, the liberal principle of the "people's right to self-determination" was laid down as the prevailing international principle. In terms of international law, the principle was institutionalised by the establishment of the *League of Nations* in 1919. However, the reorganisation of Europe after World War I was not only democracy's victory, but even more so the victory of totalitarianism, nationalism and racism. With Lenin (1870-1924) at the helm, Russia evolved from 1917 according to socialist principles; with Mussolini (1883-1945) as the front figure, Italy was from 1922 reformed according to fascist principles; and with Hitler (1889-1945) as Führer, Germany was from 1933 restructured according to national socialist principles.

For the Social Democrats, the relations between socialism, democracy, and nation-state were in general an unresolved ideological issue up until World War I. First of all, was it possible to implement socialism within the framework of liberal democracy? Secondly, was it possible to implement socialism in only one nation-state without a concurrent world-revolution? In different ways, two events helped reveal the answer: the outbreak of World War I and the Russian Revolution. World War I was to many Social Democrats a painful realisation of how national interests dominated international relationships. The war showed that national brotherhood came before international solidarity. The faith in internationalism was delivered a blow from which it never recovered. At the same time, the Russian Revolution in 1917 finally split socialism into social democratic and communistic factions. The essential difference between the two factions was their relation to democracy. While the Leninist version of communism sought to implement socialism through a dictatorship of the proletariat, the Social Democrats wanted to implement socialism through democracy.

In Denmark, the leading social democrat Frederik Borgbjerg (1866-1936) first formulated the ideological consequences of the experiences leading up to the commencement of World War I. In a speech in August 1914, he emphasised that the national community was a prerequisite for the international community, and that the aim must be to establish national social democratic parties. After World War I, the social democratic strategy in Denmark and the rest of Scandinavia was laid out in order to create socialism on a national and democratic foundation; the democratic nation-state was now the main framework for building the social state.

Ever since World War I, the strategy of the Social Democrats in Denmark, and in Scandinavia in general, was to work towards grounding socialism on national soil. When the Social Democrats came into power in 1929 the creation of a nation as the people's home took place. It was the Swedish social democrat Per Albin Hansson (1885-1944) who in 1928 made 'the People's Home' *(Folkhemmet)* a key notion in the party's ideology. In Denmark the ideological motto among Social Democrats under the leadership of Prime Minister, Thorvald Stauning (1873-1942), became 'Denmark for the people' *(Danmark for folket)*, which was used as the title of a new party manifesto in 1934.

In the manifesto the struggle between different political ideologies is clearly reflected: "The social Democratic Party's

Executive Committee will continue to advocate a policy based on law. We categorically reject attempts to deprive the people of its right of co-determination. We fight the dictatorship movement that bears the name of communism, and we fight the various forms of fascism that have also now appeared in this country" (*Danmark for folket* 1934).

Stauning's greatest ideological feat was to make the Social Democrats accept the notion of the people as politically correct. The three connotations of *people* – people as a political, cultural and social category – made it possible to talk on behalf of the democratic state, the entire population, as well of the working class, whose interests the party held in high esteem. By translating the class concept into popular terms, the Social Democratic Party established itself as the large party of the people. In contrast to the racist interpretation of the term people adopted by National Socialism, the Social Democratic Party developed a popular concept that was based on a social and democratic interpretation.

This combination is a key to the understanding of the concept *nation* that was gradually developed by the Social Democrats in the inter-war period. The strategy was to create as strong a tie as possible among the social, the national and the democratic sphere. The national and democratic foundation of Denmark's society should be strengthened by means of a social rather than a military build-up. In order to protect the country from external threats, neutrality should be the basis of the foreign policy. Likewise, social policy should secure the country internally by facilitating solidarity; this would be effected by bringing those in the worst positions to acknowledge the state and the society as theirs.

When Borgbjerg became Minister of Educational Affairs in 1929, he considered it his task to develop a school system that could fortify democratic socialism. It is remarkable that Borgbjerg wholeheartedly supported the Grundtvigian liberal tradition in Danish school legislation. Not all Social Democrats, however, had such a liking for Grundtvig as Borgbjerg. Julius Bomholt (1896-1969) feared that individualism, if it was not countered, would undermine the essential solidarity, and hence wanted to strengthen democratic socialism through cultural class struggle. Bomholt's solution was to understand freedom as class liberation rather than freedom of the individual. This ideology was, to a large extent, the basis of Roskilde Folkehøjskole that was founded by the *Workers Enlightenment Association* in 1930. To Bomholt it was clear that the most important class struggle was the cultural class struggle. If capital managed to 'bourgeoisify' the workers, the battle would be lost.

In the inter-war years Social Democrats were not only embedded in a struggle for strengthening the workers culture, but also the link between social welfare and democracy. It was not only the Nordic Social Democrats that stressed social welfare. Soviet communism and German National Socialism had distinct ideas about the welfare state (Mazower 1999:76–103). The combination of socialism and nationalism was a common element in Stalin's communism, Hitler's National Socialism, and Stauning's socialism, but only in Stauning's version were these elements combined with democracy. Stauning's greatest political achievement was the so-called Kanslergade settlement, whereby the leading parties entered a historic settlement on a series of social reforms intended to counter the social consequences of the Great Depression. The settlement was signed on 30 January 1933, the very same day that Hitler was appointed Reich Chancellor in Berlin.

Hartvig Frisch (1893-1950), a leading social democratic thinker, draws in his book *Plague over Europe* from 1933 a clear front against communism, fascism and nazism. Frisch equated the three isms as being anti-democratic and a threat to the democratic system. In particular, Hartvig Frisch devoted considerable attention to the labour movement's position in the ideological struggle. For the working class in Denmark, it was a matter of holding firmly onto Nordic democracy, whose essence, according to Hartvig Frisch, was that the nation is seen as the starting point for co-operation between workers, farmers and other population groups. "It was the peasant farmers in the Nordic countries that had led parliamentarianism to victory and created political democracy – it is to their credit. It is the labour movement that has built on this platform and forged the foundation for social democracy" (Frisch 1933).

When the Nazis assumed power in Germany in 1933, the struggle between different interpretations of the concept people was intensified. In *Mein Kampf* Hitler made race the constituting principal of a people in Germany and in some sense in all of Europe. It is the task of the nation-state to protect people, but while that meant the protection of a lingual community to Fichte, to Hitler the protection of a biological organism was the aim. The nation-state should, according to Hitler, secure the future of the race, "in relation to which the individual's desire and egoism should not matter the least and whose only duty is to yield" (Hitler 1966:27). The race ideology of national socialism was extreme, but it was nurtured by thoughts that were already wide-spread both before and after World War I. Specially in Germany, the internal struggle within the concept people turned into a nightmare, when German *Volk* – representative par excellence of the 'people' as a whole body – sought to eliminate the Jews forever (Agamben 1995:179).

IV. Democratic Welfare State

1945-1989

Jens Otto Krag was the strategist behind the Social Democrats welfare policy after World War II. As Prime Minister he later convinced the Social Democrats to haul Denmark into the EEC, which became a reality on 2 October 1972.

© ABA. Photo: Henrik Nielsen.

Demos-strategy

What many had feared happened on 9 April 1940, when Denmark was occupied by Germany. Denmark surrendered with virtually no military resistance. (Munch was the Foreign Minister at this point). Shortly after, a national coalition government was established, which governed with broad electoral support in collaboration with the occupying power until 29 August 1943. The government, however, was quickly confronted with demands from the occupying power that could not be met without violating central principles of law. In this way, the policy of collaboration raised fundamental questions about the relationship between democracy and rule of law. Can democracy defend compromising with injustice and thus take co-responsibility for such injustice when the aim is to avoid that which is worse? How deep can democracy cut into the rule of law before the very idea and legitimacy of democracy becomes lost? After a series of popular strikes in the summer 1943, the policy of collaboration came to an end on 29 August 1943, after which time support for the resistance movement increased dramatically. In the final phase of the war, the Danish resistance movement contributed to changing the image of Denmark – both to the outside world and among ourselves.

The collapse of the policy of collaboration placed the Danish Jews in a far more precarious position than earlier. Until September 1943, the policy of collaboration had effectively protected the Danish Jews at a time when the systematic implementation of holocaust had long begun in German-controlled areas of Europe. When rumours of an approaching action against the Danish Jews began to circulate in September 1943, the majority of them sought refuge among non-Jewish friends and acquaintances. The fleeing Jews were to a large extent helped by fellow Danish citizens and sailed to Sweden before the German operation on 2 October. The rescue of the Danish Jews from the Holocaust has since stood as the Danes' finest hour. The arrest operation contributed to changing people's view of the war: from regarding it as a national struggle against Germany to regarding it as a struggle against Nazism.

The occupation raised the question: Could the Danish nation be preserved even though the Danish state was occupied? The leading national strategist of this battle was the theologian Hal Koch (1904-1963). He did not pay too much attention to the contrast between Denmark and Germany. According to his interpretation, World War II was not so much a war between nations as it was a war between political systems – a war between democracy and totalitarianism. In the struggle against the occupiers, it was crucial to strengthen and maintain a democratic mindset in Denmark, particularly in the youth (Korsgaard 1997:348–57; Korsgaard 2004:452–6).

In the fall of 1940, Koch was asked to be the president of the newly established Danish Youth Association, whose aim was to counter the impact of Nazism on young Danes. He stipulated that the aim of the association should be to politizise Danish youth. In disassociating itself from the common view of 'culture' as unifying and 'politics' as dividing, Koch's understanding of politics came as a surprise to a lot of people.

"Usually I would be one to caution people who talk too much about 'culture', as it is a very dangerous word. It leads to abstract talk of 'Our thousand-year legacy,' 'what it means to be Danish' and the 'deep cultural values.' It is things like these that make Nazism flourish. If you dig down into the cultural phere it shows, that "culture does not unify, it divides." And that is the way it should be. There is a vast difference between cultures in the life of a peasant woman from western Jutland as opposed to a lady of the bourgeoisie in Copenhagen. What is common is to be found elsewhere: 'When it comes down to it, it is the political sphere that ties us together'" (Koch 1942:16). That is to say democracy.

Nazism and fascism confronted Koch with a question: What could keep the Danish society together? When the anti-democratic ideologies began advocating national-cultural values, it was necessary, according to Koch, to change strategy and emphasise *demos* at the expense of *ethnos* as the binding or unifying factor. Political-democratic values should be strengthened instead of national-cultural values. The key term in Koch's theory of democracy was for that reason not a national-cultural mindset, but rather the notion of democratic fellow citizenship.

Koch is an example of the general tendency that showed up after the war, giving low priority to the *ethnos* and high priority to the *demos*. At that same time, an extension of the notion of democracy was under way. It is perhaps illuminating to refer to David Held, who distinguishes between two types of democracy, a *protective* and a *developmental* democracy (Held 1996:99–116). In a protective democracy the most important task of society is to protect fundamental human rights, such as the right of property. That means that there are certain limits to the kind of decisions that can be made within a democracy. A majority cannot for instance make an act to considerably reduce the right of property, or of freedom of speech or the press. In a developing democracy, democracy is regarded as being more than a fixed set of rules. Democracy is something that needs to evolve in order to include economic, social, and cultural dimensions as well.

In Denmark, the preparations for the transition from *protective* democracy to *developmental* democracy was made during World War II, and then brought to bear by the Social Democrats after the war. While liberal democracy emphasised the protection of the individual's freedom *from* the acts of state, social democracy emphasised a realisation of economic and social rights *via* the state (Slagstad 1987:257). There is a marked difference in state size in these two models of democracy: on the one hand we have an idea of a highly restricted authority, and on the other, an expansive state-regulation wherein the accomplishment of political aims determines the extension of the state.

In Denmark, Koch became the leading advocate of the *demos*-strategy. In an important article, "The Hour of Reckoning" from December 1943, he stressed vehemently that the *demos*-strategy would be the template for the politics of the post-war period. These politics must be based on strong ties between the social, the national, and the democratic sphere, he wrote. "The post-war period's real – not to say only – problem is whether national solidarity can be exchanged with an actual economic community where the burdens dealt with match the abilities to carry – not the ability to shove ... We have to demand that future economic and social solidarity in every respect turn out so that we in the D.U. (*Danish Youth Organisation)* can retain the same praise of solidarity and community – retain it even when we are faced with the pressure from within" (Fonsmark 1990:54–5).

With this article, Koch clearly drew out his position on the priority of the social and the economic sphere in the post-war period. He reckoned with acknowledgement that everybody was in the same boat by virtue of a national and cultural community. His position was that a national 'boat-community' required a prior social and economic community; and a national community could only be established if there was a just distribution of goods. He therefore proposed a radical change in the understanding of the national sphere. The national subject had to be made of social and economic content rather than spiritual and cultural. The welfare state can be seen as an incarnation of the view that democracy is not only a form of politics, but a form of society and a form of life as well.

Koch referred several times to Russia as an ideal when he talked about social and economic rights, even though he simultaneously maintained a critical distance from the political system. In *What is democracy?* from 1945 he wrote: "Soviet-Russia does not yet seem to have reached democracy politically. On the other hand, one must not forget that they have made an effort in another respect: They have first and foremost been preoccupied with creating an economic democracy. In that respect Western Europe still has a lot to learn" (Koch 1970:25–6).

In Koch's view, the financial crisis of the 1930's had been a vital factor in the advance of totalitarian systems and the crisis of democracy. He therefore did not believe that a political democracy could last without a concomitant social and economic democracy. Koch became one of the great ideologists in the building of the welfare state after World War II.

Welfare as Defence

Due to the outbreak of the Cold War, Denmark joined NATO in 1949. It was a radical break with more than a hundred years of neutrality. This shift in defence policy and matters of national security was linked to a demand for a higher defence budget, which was a particular sore spot for the Social Democrats. Confronted with NATO and the American government's demand for increased defence budgets, the Social Democratic leaders were nevertheless successful in winning sympathy for their views; that welfare should not be regarded as a luxury, but as an essential element in the defence strategy against Communism. The prime-minister-to-be Jens Otto Krag (1914-1978) was one of the leading strategists accountable for conjuring up the image that displayed the communists inside Europe as the greatest threat. Countering that threat primarily required a struggle against communism inside the country, and this struggle could not be won by military means; it required social means.

"Moderation must be displayed in the demands on defence in the European countries. What good does it do us to arm Europe with a strong defence if at the same time we lower the standard of living, which will allow the internal communism to flourish?" And in addition he said: "What good does it do us to have a defence that keeps the communism away from the main gate, if it comes sneaking in the back?" (Lidegaard 2001:425).

The Social Democrats argued national security from this perspective, claiming that increased welfare would rob communism of its strongest weapon: social impoverishment, ignorance, and misery. When this strategy was developed, the Soviet Union still had social and material results to show for itself that were alluring to many in Western Europe. The Social Democrats' argument was that if the population's living conditions were not improved quickly, no armaments or ideological war, no matter how strong, would be enough to remove the attraction of communism. For that reason it was vital that capitalism was given a social face. And in reverse, if capitalism could show a bigger production and a distribution of goods broad enough to supply everyone, it would provide a greater security than any military build-up could ever do. The Social Democrats managed to get some sympathy for their point of view in the American government, and were therefore able to continue their old social and educational policies along with the new defence politics and matters of national security.

With the acceptance of welfare as a form of defence, it was possible for Denmark, with the Social Democrats as the primary advocates, to establish a strong welfare state.

The Welfare State

With World War II coming to an end, it was time to breathe life into some of the thoughts on the organisation of society and democracy that had been developed during the war. Many of the political controversies that had characterised the period from 1920 to 1940 were minimised considerably thanks to the war's need for collaboration. There was for that reason a strong political agreement to solidify democracy, and it was intended to come about through a democratisation of new areas of society. This point of view came out most clearly in the Social Democrats' party platform "The Future Denmark", which was introduced in 1945. The platform emphasised that "democracies have to show, that not only can they win the war, but that they can also provide safety" (*Fremtidens Danmark* 1945:6). Democracy should include not only the political field, but the economic field as well: "Democratisation must be followed through. Concurrent with the completion of the political democracy, economic democracy must be realised" (*Fremtidens Danmark* 1945:14). Economic democracy was a catchword with broad appeal just after the war. Even five of the parliament's seven political parties used the term in their political platforms. After the war democracy became a vogue word. In order to strengthen the feeling of democratic co-citizenship, citizens should be ensured a number of economic and social rights.

The Welfare State can be seen as the materialisation of the

view that democracy should provide the government with a 'social' form. In the core of this form of government lies the ideas that the state must counter the asymmetry generated by the market and establish a state of symmetry among its citizens. The social rights must be extended to rectify the inequalities brought about by the market.

An important prerequisite for the party's welfare policy was an economic policy based on two pillars: plan and market. The Social Democrats' congressional manifesto of 1953 stated that *regulating* methods as well as open competition should be used. With this manifesto, the structure was laid out for the production sector that would finance the construction of the welfare state. The later Social Democratic Party Prime Minister, Jens Otto Krag, was convinced that it was possible to create unprecedented wealth and economic drive through a proper control of the national economy. Crisis and massive unemployment were not uncontrollable natural phenomena, but were merely social phenomena that could be countered through state planning and political control. Their reason for the confidence in the state as a regulating factor was without a doubt the financial crisis and the massive unemployment of the inter-war period. After 1945, there was sympathy for the point of view that public intervention in the market economy should protect society from problems like those of the inter-war period. The economy should be placed under political restrictions.

The Social Democrats were the main driving force giving the state a social form. Inspired by J.M. Keynes (1883-1946), young economists with social democratic affiliations drew up the blueprint of the welfare state. The welfare state should: Secure the basic social and economic safety of every citizen; provide everybody with decent housing and access to health care as well as education; and replace poverty-relief with the right to receive aid. Further, democratic citizenship was to be based on certain rights that would be valid for everyone without regard to social or economic status. It was important to experience "the feeling of being a citizen with rights," Jens Otto Krag wrote in reference to the law on public pensions of 1956, which guaranteed everybody a basic amount of money. And he added, "Democratic freedom now has a social content" (Krag 1956). The underlying political idea was that social rights ensure an equality of status in relation to the state and an independence from the market.

A key element in the social democratic model was the concept of the 'friendly state'. The strategic aspect of the model was a strong and expansive public sector, a strategy at odds with a series of liberal ideas and Grundtvigian concepts, which, as mentioned, was based on a fundamental state-scepticism. But during and following World War II, a number of Grundtvigians like Hal Koch began to approach the social democratic perspective on the state. The establishment of the welfare state did not lead to a complete abandonment of liberal ideas, however. The welfare state – as opposed to a totalitarian system – was ultimately based on a liberal view of the state. Of course, the state did to a large extent take over the roles of the family and private institutions as up-bringers and norm-setters, but this upbringing and disciplining was combined with individual participation and influence. Furthermore, it seems that the welfare state's individualisation of rights has furthered the general individualisation in the last decade's progression of society. According to the Danish political scientist Ove Kaj Pedersen (1948-), the welfare state has managed to allow the individual to assume responsibility for the community without intruding upon the individual's rights to freedom. On the contrary, these rights have been furthered. Making the individual responsible for the community is a needed new form of regulation which is founded on individualisation (Pedersen 1994:125).

Education and Democracy

After World War II the discussion about democracy is in Denmark linked to two names: the theologian Hal Koch, who in 1945 published *What is democracy?* and the lawyer Alf Ross (1899-1979), who wrote *Why democracy?* published in 1946. In the two books, two different perceptions of democracy are presented.

The difference between Hal Koch and Alf Ross concerns a substantial idea versus a formal idea of what constitutes a people: Is it the *demos* or the constitution that is the determining factor? For Hal Koch democracy is first and foremost a *way of life*, at the heart of which is dialogue and conversation. His approach to democracy had great impact on the idea of education.

After World War II, the welfare state took on a stronger role in the upbringing of the next generation, which primarily had been the role of the family, the open associations and other private organisations. It was, however, not only a shift from the civil society to state institutions but also a shift from a national to a democratic upbringing. Before the war, the debate had revolved around what kind of upbringing the nation needed. After the war, the issue became what kind of upbringing democracy needed. Two national institutions, Denmark's Radio and the public school were entrusted with educating and forming the individual into a democratic citizen.

The Social Democrats regarded education as a boon that should be more justly distributed; it was also a weapon against the class structure of society. The strategy of the parties' educational politics was based on two principles. On one level, the access to education had to be democratised; on another, the educational institutions were to bring people up to be democratic citizens. After the war, when Koch was head of the Youth

Commission, the commission put out its "Report on Youth's Access to Higher Education". In the report, it was argued that the liberal principle of formal equality in education was to be realised, and that longer education should be made accessible to more children and young adults. "The desire for education to be democratised is therefore first and foremost a demand for society to uphold the inherent justice in the concept of democracy to the individual citizen regardless of standing and social position" (Korsgaard 1999:91).

The ideology of the school system during the first decade after the war was based on a social notion of equality more than a liberal notion of freedom, but it was part of the consensus in education policies that equality presupposed that the schools had autonomy in contributing to the realisation of political aims. Schools should be allowed to develop the field independent of market forces. Even though educational policies in general were considered with an eye to economic growth, this did not mean that schools had to be organised accordingly. Their primary task was not to produce economic growth, but social equality. An ideological demarcation was drawn between schools on the one hand and capital, market, and production on the other. This demarcation was supposed to ensure the undivided attention of the schools to democratic upbringing. A comprehensive school system was regarded the main resource for furthering democracy. Schools should train students in tolerance and co-operation in spite of differences in social situation and skills. In order to reach this goal, many hoped to do away with competitive aspects by, for instance, reducing the pressure from examinations.

Since the Liberals in Denmark, unlike in Norway and Sweden, played a stronger political role at the time, the introduction of a comprehensive school system took longer. In general, the Liberals accepted the idea of comprehensive schooling;

however, they did not accept the Social Democratic requirement of the long duration of comprehensive schooling (between 7 and 12 years). In 1958, a seven-year comprehensive school was introduced. During the 1960's and 1970's, the Social Democrats argued for an extension of the comprehensive schooling to nine years, introducing mixed-ability classes and abolishing exams and grades. The Liberals opposed this since they wanted to maintain the system's ability to meet the academic need of each individual child. In 1975, the Social Democratic Minister of Education, Ritt Bjerregård (1941-), succeeded in introducing a nine-year comprehensive school. However, the question of choosing the right path was still an issue after the introduction of the nine-year comprehensive school. In a report called *U 90* (educational planning until the 1990's) the Social Democrats argued for a twelve-year non-selective comprehensive school. However, this idea never made it through parliament. This has mainly to do with a change of policy during the 1980's as a result of the liberal-conservative government. However, the structure of the comprehensive school was nevertheless left untouched. After a change of government in 1991 the Social Liberal Education Minister, Ole Vig Jensen (1937-), introduced mixed ability classes in a School Act of 1993. This Act can rightly be seen in direct connection with previous acts on comprehensive schooling (Markussen 2003, Korsgaard & Wiborg 2006c).

Even though the liberals in Denmark have been more powerful than in Norway and Sweden, a nine year comprehensive school with mixed ability classes was still introduced. One reason why this could happen in all of the Scandinavian countries is the unique tradition of consensus-seeking politics between left and right. This is historically rooted in the political mobilisation of and alliance between the farmers and the workers (Esping-Andersen 1985).

V. From Nation-state to
a Federation of Nation-states
1989-

The artistic decoration of the new Reichstag in Berlin led to a fierce discussion of the notions people and population. The artist Hans Haacke believed that the old inscription "Dem Deutschen Volke" from 1916 was a strong nationalistic slogan that needed a counter point and suggested that it should be balanced by a new inscription, "Der Bevölkerung". The proposal was accepted and the parliament passed the project with 260 votes against 258.

Photos by the author.

The European House

The dream or hope of promoting peace, trade, relations and growth by means of political co-operation between European states is old. However, it was not until the *Treaty of Rome* 1957 that the idea of co-operation was effectively manifested, in that the Member States transferred important powers to common bodies, particularly with respect to the development of a 'common market'. The *Treaty of Rome* emerged from the political and cultural movements which after the horrors of World War II sought to establish the basis for peaceful co-operation in Europe.

In the wake of the fall of the Berlin Wall in 1989 and the collapse of the Soviet Union in 1991, the European Union (EU) was established. This happened in 1992 with the ratification of the *Treaty of Maastricht*, which gave the co-operation a far stronger political dimension. With the *Treaty of Maastricht*, the values upon which the co-operation is founded are accentuated. The treaty makes reference to human rights; rights which the *Treaty of Amsterdam* in 1998 highlighted as the very foundation of the Union. Furthermore, with the *Treaty of Nice* in 2000, work was done to draw up a politically binding charter of fundamental human rights, which will become legally binding with the adoption of the *Treaty of Lisbon*.

2 October 1972 became a historic day, as Denmark had a dramatic referendum on its relation to Europe. Principle-based and pragmatic attitudes to the significance of EEC membership stood in open conflict – different perceptions of sove-

reignty, of economic arguments and of democracy lined up opposite each other as never seen before. The decision to join EEC (today EU) was approved by a solid majority. Prime Minister Jens Otto Krag was the great strategist who, by an enormous effort, convinced the Social Democrats to haul Denmark into the EU. Since 1972, Danish membership of the EEC/EU has taken Danish politics and social development in a new direction. A large proportion of the legislative work involves adapting Danish law and administration to common EU standards.

The EU is more than an international organisation based on international law and diplomatic relations between fully sovereign states. The co-operation in the EU differs in crucial areas from the co-operation in other international organisations. In organisations like the UN and NATO adopted rules are directed to the Member States which thereafter decide how the adopted regulation is to be transposed to national law. This is not what happens in the EU. There, a large proportion of the decisions have a direct impact on citizens and companies in the Member States. In other words, EU regulation has the same status in the national legal system as legislation adopted by the Danish Parliament and ratified by the government. This system has given the European Court strong authority. Perhaps more than any other institution, the court has directed the EU towards federalism and aided the partnership beyond what is normally expected from an international partnership.

However, the European judicial-political process seems to have reached a phase where the integration cannot be continued without new energy – without a European *demos*, without a European citizen. But is it realistic to believe that a European society can be created based on trans-national and democratic ideas and a cosmopolitan culture? According to Anthony D. Smith (1939-), no European *demos* can be established when there is no European *ethnos*. Democracy is not only in need of a *demos* that can be identified, but also an *ethnos* that can be symbolised. Jürgen Habermas (1929-) has a more positive outlook on the possibilities of a European *demos*. The separation between church and state founded the secularised state as we know it today. A separation between *demos* and *ethnos* can likewise start the development of a cosmopolitan democracy in Europe. Europe is in many ways faced with the same challenge that the United Monarchy faced in 1848, where the main issue was whether or not it was possible to institute a free and common constitution within the existing multinational monarchy. Denmark did, as we know, not succeed, and whether Europe will is still an open question.

Migration

While migration for centuries has been from Europe towards other continents, the flow is now reversed. Denmark is thus distancing itself from the ideal of coinciding state, people, language and culture. A policy of cultural assimilation is obviously not in accord with multiculturalism and its respect for cultural liberty. The relation between culture and politics is still an issue in the multiculturalism debate. *Multiculturalism* does not refer to politics; it only refers to culture. It is, consequently, easier for the multiculturalists to argue for the acknowledgement of cultural diversity than it is for them to defend the democratic constitutional state. *Multiculturalism* does not include a *demos* the way the *people* does. *People* has, unlike *multiculturalism*, three connotations consisting of a political, a cultural and a social sense.

The Danish judicial and political system was originally founded on the allocation of rights to the individual, not the group. This still holds, at least in theory, in regard to the law on founding private independent schools. In practice, however, religious and cultural minorities establish private schools as if the law allocates cultural rights to groups. Minority schools are seldom based on a coinciding *demos* and *ethnos* as in the public school, but that is not a problem if the *demos* – explicitly or implicitly – play a part in the school's activity. The problem only arises when the role of the *demos* is ignored.

Children's socio-ethical upbringing is a delicate issue, especially when it concerns where to draw the line between the democratic constitutional state and cultural autonomy. Can a democratic state undermine cultural and religious autonomy in its attempt to secure democracy through education? Or can the democratic virtue of freedom be undermined if the state is idle and does not secure children's democratic upbringing? The constitution provides the parents with the right to establish free schools, but which duties do the parents have with regard to the constitution?

Around 2000 doubts were raised as to whether or not Islamic private schools lived up to the responsibility of teaching their students how to live in the Danish democracy. In 2002 this led to Parliament making it a legal requirement for private schools to prepare their students to live in a society of freedom and democracy. Since then, the Minister of Education has closed several Islamic private schools because the Ministry concluded that they did not live up to the educational standards of public schools (Korsgaard 2004:530-37).

The Islamic private schools, as they are usually called (even though Arabic private schools are not necessarily Islamic), are organised within the Danish Private School Association, whose core comprises the old Grundtvigian free schools. This association between Grundtvigian private schools and the ethnic private schools is no coincidence. No doubt this comes from the

Grundtvigian legacy of defending a minority's right to establish schools founded in and for their own culture.

That multiculturalism and multi-religiosity is becoming a societal condition has evidently brought back the following issue: What are the basic values of society, and which values is the educational system going to maintain and develop?

In 2000, the then Minister of Education Margrethe Vestager (1968-), wrote a text called *Values in reality*. By *Values in reality* the schism between Rousseau and Herder is recapitulated – the schism between a contractual agreement (political) and a lingual community (cultural) as the fundamental constitution of society.

On the Way towards a New Policy of Education

The construction of a national identity is impossible without the humanities, particularly national literature and national history. Up until 1970, the humanities were designed to administer history so that it would not loose its identity and form in its encounter with the next generation. But this system collapsed to a large degree around 1970. This happened with the implementation of the principle of choice, which in one stroke put the students in charge of the subjects' tradition and the canon. This was a break with a long tradition for a strong historical approach to national literature. Just like national literature, national history has been challenged by implementing choice as a pedagogical principle. Even though the genre has been challenged throughout the last three decades it was not until Uffe Østergaard's (1945-) work *Europas ansigter* (1992) (*The Faces of Europe*) and Søren Mørch's (1933-) *Den sidste Danmarkshistorie* (1996) (*The Last Danish History*) that professional historians have related their works with Denmark's position in Europe more explicitly, and therefore had to reconsider the socio-historical premise of writing Danish history at all.

Popular narration as a means of general education is disintegrating as well. The rostrum has lost its aura as the place of popular truth and authority. The days are long gone when crowds of young in the hundreds sat listening to popular narration. Music and artistic subjects have, in the course of the last 30 years, replaced history and literature as the main subjects of the folk high school. About the time the 'principle of choice' led to a radical reform of the humanities' history in the universities, it also in the folk high school led, to a break with its historical tradition.

The breakdown of this tradition may be an indication of a new strategy reconfiguring the educational system by shifting the institutions' focal points from the perpetuation of general culture to the promotion of skills or qualifications in a post-modern globalised network state.

The 'know-how state' is a post-industrial state type, which, in contrast to the industrial state, is determined by division of knowledge – in addition to division of labour. Former Minister of Finance Thorkild Christensen (1899-1989) already pointed out in 1971 that the growth of knowledge must be taken into account "in every attempt to understand the progress" (Kristensen 1971:15). Knowledge contributes to production in two ways: by being incorporated in people and by being incorporated in machinery. This material and individual incorporation of knowledge by means of information technologies seem to be characteristic of globalisation. With such a qualitative shift we can for the first time in history organise our production – not only the trade – within a transnational framework. The configuration of the 'know-how state' has caused a radical lingual shift. On the rhetorical level, education has been replaced with lifelong lifewide learning. This means that the distinction between school and society disappears, leading to vast consequences for the humanistic notion of general education. General education is historically based on a notion of the school as a self-sustaining community. When life – including work – is subjugated to a demand for life-long training, the clear distinction between school and work is blurred and the basis for general education disintegrates. The new media help blur the distinction between school and society, furthering individualisation.

Withdrawing mentally from a community seems to be interwoven with individualisation. The individualisation Luther commenced 500 years ago helped dispose of the medieval world order and establish the prince-state. The individualisation furthered by people like Rousseau, Kant, Fichte and Grundtvig 200 years ago weakened the power of lineage and household that supported 'the nation'. Today, Ulrich Beck (1944-) and Anthony Giddens (1938-) point out that individualisation assists the advancement of globalisation and vice versa.

Will the Struggle for the People Continue?

People or *Volk* lost its innocence from 1933 to 1945. After the war, it was impossible to use notions like *Völkisch* and *Volkgeist* (*popular* and *spirit of the people*). Even though the people (*folk*) did not get seriously discredited in Denmark, the emotional connotations of it were changed. The same thing happened with the notion *nation*. Hence it was normal to replace *people* with *the population of the welfare state*. The meaning of *democracy* was elaborated and it became the common replacement of the word *national*. The understanding of the word shifted from being a narrow political concept to a broader understanding of democracy, including economic, social and cultural matters.

However, the notion *people* is still a battleground for mixed and even opposing interests. Is the concept *people* opposed to the idea of European citizenship or world citizenship? Are the 'peoples' competitors or companions? Many want the word to be forgotten due to others' misuse. Others again want to maintain it, but again, for different reasons. The 2000 referendum regarding the Euro and the general election of 20 November 2001 show that it is still immensely effective to appeal to the nation's people. Søren Krarup (1937-) considers the general election of November 2001 as a breakthrough for the 'popular soul' (Krarup 2002). Jakob Andersen (1957-), on the other hand, finds the notion so 'ethnified' that it can no longer be used. He argues that 'popular rule' has to be replaced with 'homocracy' – rule of human beings (Andersen 1998:157). Ove Kaj Pedersen believes similarly that it is no longer possible *"to talk about democracy as a singular notion nor sustain the idea of one type of democracy. History has transgressed a threshold"* (Pedersen 1994:234). A new era of state configuration and nation building draws near.

Michael Hardt (1960-) and Anthony Negri (1933-) argue that a historical shift is taking place, from the nation-state to an empire without a well-defined territory nor a fixed centre of power – a network-state. With the empire, popular representation is fundamentally undermined. This has severe consequences for the notion of democracy, where the fundamental principle is the sovereignty of the people. Democracy will free itself from the nation and the people and tie itself to the empire where the 'multitude' will replace the people as the heart of democracy (Hardt and Negri 2002:326-336).

In opposition to Hardt and Negri, John Rawls (1912-2002) retains *peoples* as an essential notion in his political philosophy. In *The Law of Peoples* (1999) Rawls argues that it is not enough to have a theory about states and human rights, it is also necessary to have a theory about peoples. According to Rawls a people is united by 'common sympathies'; it is more than a collection; it constitutes a group sharing certain moral and political ideas that are capable of being articulated into a theory of justice. The members of a people are not defined by the state; on the contrary, they control the government that represents them. "What distinguishes people from states – and this is crucial – is that just peoples are fully prepared to grant the very same proper respect and recognition to other people as equals" (Rawls 1999:35). Inspired by Kant, Rawls argues for an extension of the judicial principles established on a national level to be established in the international society. He thus takes up Kant's idea from *The Eternal Peace* where Kant sought to tame the international society of wolves and suggested a world-citizenship of the democratic states' populations. Rawls' utopia is a political idea that goes beyond the limits of political and practical possibility – at least short-term – but which can function as a normative ideal for long-term policies.

The artistic decoration of the new *Reichstag* in Berlin led to a fierce discussion of the notions *people* and *population*. The artist Hans Haacke believed that the old inscription "*Dem Deutschen Volke*" from 1916 was a strong nationalistic slogan that needed a counter point and suggested that it should be balanced by a new inscription, "*Der Bevölkerung*". The adherents supported the suggestion because 'the German people' was an ethnic notion that did not include everybody in Germany. The opponents warned against watering down the notion of *the people* because the German democracy needed a *demos* – a people. The proposal was accepted and the parliament passed the project with 260 votes against 258. The piece was inaugurated on 12 September 2000 (Korsgaard 2004:561-63).

This story of 'people' shows that there are many different conceptions of the notion at work. *People* is a dynamic concept.

I believe it is important to preserve the idea of a Danish people, and such an idea does not in itself conflict with the notion of a European people. This, however, requires that we give up the view that it is possible to be part of only one people. *People* is an idea that can take many shapes. The future depends on the interpretations we have of the people.

A Closing Remark and a Question Mark

Looking back on the last 500 years, the development of Danish identity and society has been shaped by different interpretations of the concept people. Roughly speaking: from the time of the Reformation up to implementing the idea of democracy, the notion people was not associated with a sovereign nation, but rather with household. In this sense people was always part of a hierarchic structure that was determined by a relation between a master and a people. The notion was used in relation to the master of a house, the king of a country, as well as the lord God. During the period of absolute monarchy, the word people in particular was used as a designation for a social category; a distinction was drawn between 'upstairs' and 'downstairs', between master and servants.

As part of the process towards democracy, the term people was introduced as a sovereignty concept in a new state structure. Since the mid-1800's, people's sovereignty and Danish identity has been promoted by political programs of three different classes or social movements: The national liberal movement, the peasant or grundtvigian movement, and the labor movement, which successively have left their mark on the development of the Danish society

The national liberals caused the shift that replaced the monarch with the people as the center of the symbolic order. Their approaches to democracy were a top-down perspective. However, the National Liberals lost considerable political and cultural influence in the wake of the defeat in 1864, which had a significant impact on the future evolution of democracy in Denmark.

In the power vacuum that appeared after 1864 the peasant movement shaped by popular Grundtvigianism was the only movement with any general appeal. In contrast to the National Liberals, the Grundtvigians regarded civil society, not the state, as the complement of the people; 'popular', in the Danish context, became almost synonymous with what is understood as external to the state in the liberal tradition. This move from state to civil society was more than just an ideological shift; it was also a shift dictated by the fact that, up until 1901, landowners and the king had power to block access to the government.

The labor movement and Social Democrats clarified the notions *people* and *nation* during World War I. The nation was not just a stage in historical development that belongs to the past; rather, the nation was the basis for the realization of democracy and socialism. The link between democracy and sociality, developed by the Social Democrats during the interwar period, came to be the future conception of the nation. The developed concept of people was fundamentally different from the Nazi notion of people. It was a conception based not on a race-ideology, but on a combination of social and political ideology.

During World War II a kind of national compromise was created between the liberal and the social democratic conceptions of state, nation, people and democracy. This compromise became the foundation of the creation in the postwar period of the welfare state, governed by socialistic as well as liberal ideas. Welfare and Danishness became one and the same. To be Danish was to identify oneself with the Danish welfare project.

During the last fifty years the welfare system, more than anything else, is what has grounded the nation in the heart of the Danish people. Today, however, we are confronted with the alarming question: Is this way of grounding the nation losing its power as a result of expanding globalization, individualization and migration? (Korsgaard 2006a:157f).

References

Agamben, Giorgio (1995): *Homo Sacer. Sovereign Power and Bare Life*. Standford University Press.

Andersen, Jacob (1998): *Fra folkestyre til fællesstyre*. Gyldendal, Copenhagen.

Clausen, H. N. (1870): *Det videnskabelige Livs Forhold til det borgerlige Frihedsliv*. G.E.C Gad, Copenhagen.

The Danish Democracy Canon (2008). Published by the committee established for the purpose of drawing up a democratic canon and the Danish Ministry of Education. Copenhagen.

Esping-Andersen, Gøsta (1985): *Politics against Market: The Social Democratic Road to Power*. Princeton University Press, Princeton.

Fonsmark, Henning (1990): *Historien om den danske utopi*. Gyldendal, Copenhagen.

Fremtidens Danmark (1946): Fremad: København.

Gellner, Ernest (1994): *Nation and Nationalism*. Blackwell, Oxford UK & Cambridge USA (1983).

Goldschmidt, Meir (1849): *Nord og syd*, vols. 9 and 10. Copenhagen.

Greenfeld, Liah (1992): *Nationalism. Five Roads to Modernity*. Harvard University Press, Cambridge, Massachusetts.

Grundtvig, N.F.S. (1909): *Udvalgte skrifter*, vol. 9. Nordisk Forlag, Copenhagen.

Grundtvig, N.F.S. (1965): *Taler på Marienlyst Højskole 1856-71*. Gyldendal, Copenhagen.

Grundtvig, Svend (1968): *Grundtvigs skoleverden I-II*. Published by K.E. Bugge, Copenhagen.

Hardt, Michael og Anthonio Negri (2001): "Globalization and Democracy". In *Democracy Unrealized. Documenta 11_Platform 1*. Hatje Cantz Publishers: Germany.

Held, David (1996): *Models of Democracy*. Polity Press, Cambridge.

Hitler, Adolf (1966): *Min kamp*. Jørgen Paludans forlag, Copenhagen (1925).

Højrup, Thomas (2002): *Dannelsens didaktik*. Museum Tusculanum, Copenhagen.

Kant, Immanuel (1993): *Oplysning, historie, fremskridt*. Slagmark, Aarhus.

Kant, Immanuel (2000): *Om pædagogik*, Forlaget Klim. Aarhus (1803).

Koch, Hal (1942): *Dagen og vejen*. Westermann, Copenhagen.

Koch, Hal (1970): *Hvad er demokrati?* Gyldendal, Copenhagen (1945).

Korsgaard, Ove (1997): *Kampen om lyset. Dansk voksenoplysning gennem 500 år*. Gyldendal, Copenhagen.

Korsgaard, Ove (1999): *Kundskabskapløbet. Uddannelse i videnssamfundet*. Gyldendal, Copenhagen.

Korsgaard, Ove (2004): *Kampen om folket. Et dannelsesperspektiv på dansk historie gennem 500 år*. Gyldendal, Copenhagen.

Korsgaard, Ove (2006a): "The Danish Way to Establish the Nation in the Hearts of the People". In John L. Campell, John A. Hall, and Ove Kaj Pedersen (Eds.): *National Identity and the Varieties of Capitalism. The Danish Experience*. McGill-Queen's University Press.

Korsgaard, Ove (2006b): "Giving the Spirit a National Form: From Rousseau's advise to Poland to Habermas' advice to the European Union". In *Educational Philosophy and Theory*. Vol. 38, nr. 2/2006.

Korsgaard & Wiborg (2006c) "Grundtvig – the Key to Danish Education?" In *Scandinavian Journal of Education*, vol. 50, no. 3.

Krag, Jens Otto (1956): Feature Article in *Socialdemokraten* 23 October.

Krarup, Søren (2002): "Det kulturradikale sammenbrud". In *Politiken* 16 March.

Kristensen, Thorkild (1971): "Kundskab som produktionsfaktor". In *Nationaløkonomisk Tidsskrift*, vol. 109.

Lidegaard, Bo (2001): *Jens Otto Krag*, vol. 1. Gyldendal, Copenhagen.

Lyhne, Vagn (2000): *Lærermesteren. Kant og oplysningstidens pædagogik*. Klim, Aarhus.

Malling, Anders (1978): *Dansk Salmehistorie*, bd. VIII. Schultz Forlag, Copenhagen.

Markussen, Ingrid (1988): *Visdommens lænker*. Landbohistorisk Selskab, Copenhagen.

Markussen, Ingrid (2003): "Dannelsessyn og drivkræfter bag enhedsskolens fremvækst". In Rune Slagstad, Ove Korsgaard & Lars Løvlie (Eds.): *Dannelsens forvandlinger*. Pax Forlag: Oslo.

Mazower, Mark. (1999): *Dark Continent. Europe's Twentieth Century*. Alfred A. Knopf: New York.

Mørch, Søren (1996): *Den sidste Danmarkshistorie*. Gyldendal, Copenhagen.

Nielsen, Johs. (1979): *Genrejsningshåb og undergangsangst. Dansk forsvarspolitik mellem 1864 og 1870 og folkestyrets første forsvarsordning*. Odense Universitetsforlag, Odense.

O'Leary, Brendan (2001): "The elements of Right-Sizing and Right-Peopling the State". In Brendan O'leary, Ian S. Lustick and Thomas Gallaghy (Eds.): *Right-Sizing the State: the Politics of Moving Borders*. Oxford University Press, New York.

Pedersen, Ove Kaj (1994): *Demokratiets lette tilstand.* Spektrum, Copenhagen.

Petersen, Niels (1984): *Kulturministeriet.* Rigsarkivet/G.E.C. Gad, Copenhagen.

Rawls, John (1999): *The Law of Peoples.* Harvard University Press: Cambridge, Massachusetts.

Ringer, Fritz K. (1969): *The Decline of the German Mandarins.* Harvard University Press: Cambridge, Massachusetts.

Rothe, Tyge (1759): Tanker om Kierlighed til Fædrelandet. Bibliotheca Danica.

Rousseau, J.J. (1991): "Considerations on the Government of Poland". In Stanley Hoffmann & David P. Fidler (Eds.): *Rousseau on International Relations.* Clarendon Press, Oxford (1772).

Rousseau, J.J. (1997): *Emile eller om opdragelse.* Borgen, Copenhagen (1762).

Schuyler, Robert Livingstone and Corinne Comstock Weston (Eds.) (1929): *Cardinal Documents in British History.* D. van Nostand Company, Princetone, New Jersey, Toronto and London.

Skovrup, Ejnar (1944): *Kolds Skoletanker.* Andelstrykkeriet, Odense.

Slagstad, Rune (1987): *Rett og Politikk.* Universitetsforlaget, Oslo.

Steenstrup, J. (1865): "Skrivelse til Den danske Folkeforening". In *Udvalg for Folkeoplysningens Fremme, 50 Aars Virksomhed* 1866-1916.

Weber, Eugen (1976): *Peasants into Frenchmen.* University Press, Stanford.

Ørsted, Anders Sandøe (1850): *Den danske Stats Opretholdelse I dens Heelhed.* Gyldendal, Copenhagen.

Østergaard, Uffe (1992): *Europas ansigter.* Rosinante, Copenhagen.

Østergaard, Uffe (2006): Denmark: "A Big Small State". In John L. Campbell, John A. Hall and Ove K. Pedersen (Eds.): *National Identity and the Variety of Capitalism. The Danish Experience.* McGill-Queen's University Press.

Index of Names

Agamben, Giorgio (1942-), Italian philosopher.

Andersen, Jakob (1957-), Danish journalist.

Aristotle (384-322), Greek philosopher.

Beck, Ulrich (1944-), German sociologist.

Berg, Christen (1829-1891), Danish politician.

Bismarck, Otto von (1815-1898), German statesman.

Bjerregård, Ritt (1941-), Danish politician.

Bomholt, Julius (1896-1969), Danish principal of a folk high school, writer, minister.

Borgbjerg, Frederik (1866-1936), Danish editor, politician, minister.

Calvin, Jean (1509-1564), Swiss reformer.

Christensen, Balthazar (1802-1882), Danish lawyer, politician.

Christensen, Hans (1781-1868), Danish farmer, politician.

Christensen, J.C. (1856-1930), Danish politician, prime minister.

Clausen, H.N. (1793-1877), Danish theologian, politician.

Engels, Friedrich (1820-1895), German theorist.

Engelstoft, Laurits (1774-1851), Danish historian.

Fichte, Johan Gottlieb (1762-1814), German philosopher.

Frisch, Hartvig (1883-1950), Danish social democratic thinker.

Foucault, Michel (1926-1984), French philosopher.

Giddens, Anthony (1938-), British sociologist.

Goldschmidt, Meir Aron (1819-1887), Danish writer.

Greenfeld, Liah (1954-), American historian.

Grundtvig, N.F.S. (1783-1872), Danish historian, vicar, writer, politician.

Gutenberg, Johannes (app. 1397-1468), German printer and inventor.

Haacke, Hans (1936-), German American artist.

Habermas, Jürgen (1929-), German sociologist.

Hansson, Per Albin (1885-1944), Swedish politician.

Hardt, Michael (1960-), American literary theorist and political philosopher.

Held, David (1951-), British political theorist.

Herder, Johann Gottfried (1744-1803), German historian and folklorist.

Hitler, Adolf (1889-1945), German dictator.

Hørup, Viggo (1841-1902), Danish lawyer, editor, politician, minister.

Jensen, Ole Vig (1936-), Danish politician.

Juel, Jens (1745-1802), Danish artist.

Kant, Immanuel (1724-1804), German philosopher.

Keynes, J.M. (1883-1946), British economist.

Koch, Hal (1904-1963), Danish theologian, principal of a folk high school.

Kold, Christen (1816-1870), founder of the first Danish free school and principal of a folk high school.

Krag, Jens Otto (1914-1978), Danish politician, prime minister

Krarup, Søren (1937-), Danish vicar, politician.

Kristensen, Thorkild (1899-1989), Danish economist, politician, secretary-general of the OECD.

Lehmann, Orla (1810-1870), Danish statesman.

Lenin, I.V. (1870-1924), Soviet head of state from 1917 to 1924

Lorenzen, Peter Hjort (1791-1845), Danish politician.

Luther, Martin (1483-1546), German reformer.

Madvig, J.N. (1804-1886), Danish philologist, politician, minister.

Monrad, D.G. (1811-1887), Danish bishop, politician, prime minister.

Moussolini, Benito (1883-1945), Italian dictator.

Munch, Peter (1870-1948), Danish historian, politician, minister.

Marx, Karl (1818-1883), German socialistic theorist.

Negri, Anthony (1933-), Italian political philosopher.

O'Leary, Brendan (1958-), Irish political scientist.

Pedersen, Chr. (d. 1554), Danish historian, writer.

Pedersen, Ove Kaj (1948-), Danish professor of public administration.

Pontoppidan, Erik (1698-1764), Danish bishop.

Ringer, Fritz K. (1931-), German American sociologist and historian.

Sander, L.C. (1756-1819), German philanthropist and writer.

Sibbern, F.C. (1785-1872), Danish philosopher.

Smith, Anthony D. (1939-), British sociologist.

Stauning, Thorvald (1873-1942), Danish politician, prime minister.

Steffens, Henrik (1773-1845), German Danish scientist and philosopher.

Sørensen, Rasmus (1799-1865), Danish lay preacher, politician.

Thomensen, Hans (1532-73), vicar.

Rawls, John (1912-2002), American political philosopher.

Reventlow, Johan Ludvig (1751-1801), Danish count, philanthropist.

Reventlow, Christian Ditlev Frederik (1748-1827), Danish count, statesman.

Rousseau, Jean-Jacques (1712-1777), French writer and philosopher.

Vestager, Margrethe (1969-), Danish politician, minister.

Wegener, Johann (1811-1883), Danish principal of a folk high school, vicar, politician.

Ørsted, A.S. (1778-1860), Danish lawyer, statesman.